THE GOSPEL-CENTERED LIFE FOR STUDENTS

MARK: HOW JESUS CHANGES EVERYTHING

John Perritt

Study Guide with Leader's Notes

New Growth Press, Greensboro, NC 27404
www.newgrowthpress.com

Cover Design: Faceout Books, faceoutstudio.com
Interior Design and Typesetting: Professional Publishing Services, christycallahan.com

ISBN: 978-1-948130-90-5 (print)
ISBN: 978-1-948130-91-2 (ebook)

Printed in the United States of America

26 25 24 23 22 21 20 19 1 2 3 4 5

This is dedicated to the youth group of Pear Orchard Presbyterian Church in Ridgeland, Mississippi. God used every student—from the leaders to those on the fringes—to help me grasp his glorious gospel more deeply. Thank you for ministering to me as I, by grace, sought to minister to you.

CONTENTS

INTRODUCTION

Why Mark? Let's start by addressing the elephant in the room: the title of this series.

I'll admit that studying the gospel of Mark in a series about "the gospel-centered life" might sound a bit redundant to some. Not only is Mark one of the four *gospels* in the New Testament, it receives that label because it details the life, death, and resurrection of Jesus Christ—who the gospel is all about. So, if the gospel is at the center of the gospel of Mark, why do we need a study helping us see what seems to be glaringly obvious?

Finding the gospel in other books of the Bible may seem a bit like uncovering a mystery, but the four gospels seem to be a straightforward account that is anything but mysterious. Jesus's life and earthly ministry are clearly laid out for all to see.

And yet, it isn't always that clear, is it?

You see, we are a people who forget. If one theme remains constant throughout the Bible, it is the fact that God's people forget the God who loves them. The God who constantly provides and constantly pursues is constantly forgotten and betrayed by the people of God.

As others have stated, we suffer from gospel amnesia. That is, we wake up every day, forgetting that we are loved and accepted by the God of all creation through the finished work of his beautiful Son, Jesus Christ. Then we look to anything and everything else to give us a secure identity, even though we have the unshakable truth of the gospel.

Therefore, it is very possible for you to read Mark's gospel and miss the gospel! So maybe a title that sounds a bit redundant isn't the worst thing.

HOW THIS STUDY IS ORGANIZED

The Gospel-Centered Life in Mark for Students is organized into twelve lessons. Since there are sixteen chapters in the gospel of Mark, these lessons will not be able to cover each passage in detail. That said, you hold in your hands a study that seeks to be faithful to God's Word and contain his truth for you.

If you were to zoom out from the book of Mark, you would notice that the first ten chapters cover approximately three years. The remaining chapters focus on just one week! A seminary professor of mine said, "I think Mark was trying to tell us something." Mark rushes through the earthly ministry of Jesus and then slows the reader down to focus on the week leading up to Christ's crucifixion. Mark is not saying that the rest of Christ's earthly ministry is unimportant—far from it—but he does place emphasis on that final week. Therefore, this study will give more attention to those chapters as well. The first five lessons each cover two chapters in Mark, while the remaining lessons slow down and cover less material.

NOTE: Because lessons 1 through 5 each cover two chapters, you will not be able to read through all the Bible text during those lessons. For this reason, you should read the chapters in Mark *before you arrive* for the lesson. These reading assignments are given at the end of the previous lesson.

If you are the group leader, part of your communication with participants should include instructions to read chapters 1 and 2 of Mark *before meeting for the first lesson.* Some participants might not do it. But if they do, it will help that first lesson go well. Assigning some simple preparation will also add a note of seriousness to your study of Mark.

HOW TO USE THIS STUDY

Like the other small group resources in this series, *The Gospel-Centered Life in Mark for Students* has a distinct focus. Your goal will be bigger than merely to study the book of Mark. You will also be learning to keep your eyes on Jesus and the good news of God's love and power to save you. And you will consider how that power takes you beyond yourself to love others—especially those who don't yet know Jesus.

Growing as a believer means you must grow in awareness of your sin and in confidence that Jesus saves you in every way from that sin. As you grow in this confidence, God will also work to reshape the desires of your heart to match his desires, which include mercy and compassion for those who are still far from him. The message of grace and hope that not-yet believers need is the same gospel message believers need to hear over and over.

The Gospel-Centered Life in Mark will help you do this in a group study. Studying with others lets you benefit from what God is also teaching them, and it gives you encouragement as you apply what you learn.

The group will be a place to share not only successes but also sins and weaknesses, so expect differences in how people participate. It's okay if some in the group are cheery while others are weary, if some "get it" quickly while others want to look more deeply, or if some are eager to share while others take it slowly. But because you'll be studying the Bible and praying together, also expect God's Spirit to work and change people—starting with you!

Each participant should have one of these study guides in order to join in reading and be able to work through the exercises during that part of the study. The leader should read through both the lesson and the leader's notes in the back of this book before the lesson begins, and and everyone should read two chapters in Mark before each of the first five lessons. Otherwise, no preparation or homework is required. Each lesson will take about an hour to complete, perhaps a bit more if your group is large, and will include these elements:

BIG IDEA. This is a summary of the main point of the lesson.

BIBLE CONVERSATION. You will read a passage from the Bible and discuss it. As the heading suggests, the Bible conversation questions are intended to spark a conversation rather than generate correct answers. In most cases, the questions will have several possible good answers and a few best answers. The leader's notes at the back of this book provide observations from the author and the study questions editor, but don't just turn there for the "right answer." At times you may want to see what the notes say, but always try to answer for yourself first by thinking about the Bible passage.

ARTICLE. This is the main teaching section of the lesson, written by the book's author.

DISCUSSION. The discussion questions following the article will help you apply the teaching to your life. Again, there will be several good ways to answer each question.

EXERCISE. The exercise will be a section of the lesson you complete on your own. You can write in the book if that helps you, or you can just think about your responses. You will then share some of what you learned with the group. If the group is large, it may help to split up to share the results of the exercise and to pray, so that everyone has a better opportunity to participate. Or you may be more comfortable sharing among just your own gender, which could be another reason to split into smaller groups.

WRAP-UP & PRAYER. Prayer is a critical part of the lesson because your spiritual growth will happen through God's work in you, not by your self-effort. You will be asking him to do that good work.

The gospel of Mark shows us Jesus. You will see his compassion for sinners and hear his determination to save you by his death and resurrection. And you will feel God's tug on the heart, which calls all who believe to come nearer still to their loving Savior.

Lesson

1

HERO OF HEROES

BIG IDEA

There is no greater authority in the world than God's Son, Jesus Christ—and there is none better.

BIBLE CONVERSATION *20 minutes*

Like an action movie, the opening chapters of the gospel of Mark are fast-paced. Mark's book tells about the life of Jesus, the Son of God who became a man. But it skips over Jesus's birth completely and moves quickly through the first years of his ministry. Mark is in a hurry to show many examples of Jesus's growing fame and his power and authority.

This lesson covers the first two chapters of Mark, so it will help for you to have read those in advance. We will read parts of the passage together now, so we can discuss them. Begin by having someone read **Mark 1:9–15** aloud, and then discuss the questions below.

When Jesus said to repent and believe the gospel, he was

- telling people what to believe
- telling people what to do, and
- telling people how to think about what's right and what's wrong.

Which of these, as people today, are you most likely to resent?

Where does Jesus seem to get the right to say such things, and how is it different from the ways other powerful people get their authority?

Pick up the story after Jesus called some fishermen to be his disciples. Someone please read **Mark 1:21–34**.

Briefly describe the kind of authority Jesus showed. Is he the sort of authority you might like to have in your life, or is he the kind you might resent? Why?

Jesus's authority eventually got challenged by the scribes and Pharisees, who were religious leaders known for their devotion to God's law. Have someone read aloud what happened, from **Mark 2:1–17**.

What do you think are some ways Jesus was planning to use his authority? Consider both his actions and things he said.

****

Gospel means "good news"—the good news of what Jesus does for us. So, as we talk about a gospel-centered life, we must notice how Jesus is the Son of God and what his purpose was in coming to earth as a man. To begin, read the following article aloud, taking turns at the paragraph breaks.

THE AUTHORITY OF THE SON OF GOD

5 minutes

What do you think when you hear the word *authority*? Maybe you would disagree with this, but I think there are negative connotations associated with that word. Whether it's in a movie or television show, we often see authority being portrayed in a bad light.

Think of how teachers and parents are portrayed in movies. We frequently see these characters depicted as out of touch or naïve. They seem foolish and lack the wisdom of the teenagers they interact with. To be sure, there are other movies that give positive portrayals of authority, but that word seems to rub us the wrong way at times.

We must also consider the fact that there are plenty of people who abuse their authority. They wield whatever authority they possess with little love and concern toward those who are under them. As Christians, we would agree this is an abuse of authority. A person with authority should not just possess power but ought to use that power for the good of others.

We clearly see in these first two chapters of Mark that Jesus is God's Son. And as we would expect, being God's Son grants a certain level of authority. But how do we see Jesus using this authority?

This authority was seen in Christ's teaching and in his ability to rebuke demons. But what I want you to see is that Jesus says he has the authority to forgive sins. The authority to forgive sins is unlike any earthly authority.

This is a power that should be staggering to us, because we are all sinners. If there is one truth the Bible clearly teaches, it is this: humanity is poisoned with sin. From Genesis 3 onward, we read of mankind's sin and depravity. Paul reiterated this in Romans 3:23: "For all have sinned and fall short of the glory of God." We all need someone with the authority to forgive us.

This is why Jesus's fame spread not only through Galilee but to the whole world. Think about it: we are here, still talking about Jesus today. Mark leaves no question that Jesus is the Son of God, and Jesus left no doubt about why he came into our world: "I came not to call the righteous, but sinners" (Mark 2:17).

What good news it is that Jesus came not to call the righteous but to love even those who were known as the worst in society! Think about your own sinful heart and the sins you are embarrassed about, the ones only you and God know. In spite of those sins, Jesus still came to call you to himself and to offer the good news of forgiveness to you.

Being God's Son and possessing the power to forgive sins places Jesus in direct authority over us. How should that make us feel? It should humble us, for sure. It should remind us that Jesus has an authority that is unlike any authority of a parent or teacher. But let us also remember that Jesus is one who does not abuse his authority like humans do. The Son of God who has all authority came to save sinners. For a group of sinners like you and me, that's an authority we can submit to.

DISCUSSION *10 minutes*

When you think of authority, do you tend to think of people who use authority well or do you think of people who abuse authority? What examples of authority come to mind, either from your life or from popular culture?

Where do you need the authority of Jesus in your life? What do you need him to use his authority to do? Try to give a specific example.

WHO'S YOUR AUTHORITY?

15 minutes

(NOTE: All of the exercises in this book will challenge you to consider how you still need to grow as a Christian. Don't let your shortcomings discourage you. We all start small. Much of God's work in your life may still be ahead of you, especially if you are young—though often it is older believers who are quickest to see and admit how much they still need to grow.)

Each of us has many authorities in life. Some are God-given authorities due to their position over us—like parents, pastors, teachers, or employers. But other people or things also have great influence over us, for good or for bad. For example, your friends might influence how you think, or you may find it hard to say no to them. Social media, a sports team, or the entertainment you consume may also dominate your thoughts, moods, and choices.

What are the authorities in your life? Pick one or two from the following list. Also think about why they are your authorities. What do they offer you? Or what do they threaten if you don't submit to them? Pick a reason or two from those lists as well. When you're done, discuss the questions at the end of the exercise with the rest of the group.

An authority in my life is ______________________________,

because it dominates my thoughts, moods, or decisions.

- Friends
- Shows or movies
- Music
- Social media interactions
- School success
- My talent at ______________________________
- Sport or activity I do: ______________________________
- Sports team I root for
- Person I admire: ______________________________
- Treasured possession: ______________________________
- Money
- Boyfriend/girlfriend
- Other: ______________________________

Submitting to this authority seems to offer me ______________

____.

- Acceptance
- A good reputation
- Escape from boredom
- A way to fit in
- Good feelings about myself
- A way to be a winner
- Comfort in life
- Security
- Excitement
- Affirmation that people like me
- Purpose and meaning
- A basic need: ______________________________
- Admiration from others
- Love
- Freedom from ______________________________
- Control of my life
- Other: ______________________________

I feel threatened by ______________________________

if I don't submit to this authority.

- Embarrassment
- Loneliness
- Being left out
- Looking like a loser
- Disapproval from ______________________________
- Failure
- Uncertainty in life
- A difficult life
- Harassment
- Unhappiness
- Rejection
- Heartbreak
- Other: ______________________________

Share some of your results with the group, and discuss them.

How is Jesus a better authority than your worldly authorities? (If you aren't sure, ask others in the group for insight.)

If you always treated Jesus as your chief authority, how would it change the way you interact with these worldly authorities?

WRAP-UP AND PRAYER *5 minutes*

The authority of Jesus brings freedom from worldly authorities. First Peter 2:16 tells us, "Live as people who are free, not using your freedom as a cover-up for evil, but living as servants of God." Jesus welcomes you into this new life with him as he promises to forgive your sin.

Now that you've seen who the true authority is—Jesus Christ—and that his authority is loving and gracious, it would be wise to pray that this true authority would take deeper root in your life. Begin by praying for this together now:

- Thank God that Jesus came to forgive and that he loves you, a sinner.
- Ask him to help you see how good Jesus is so that serving him does not feel oppressive.
- Ask him to free you from sinful desires so that you obey Jesus instead.

Before the next time you meet: Read through chapters 3 and 4 of Mark.

Lesson

2

THE GREAT TEACHER

BIG IDEA

Jesus came to teach those who would hear. Are you one of them?

BIBLE CONVERSATION *20 minutes*

Whether you enjoy school or don't like it much may depend on your teachers. Much of Mark 3 and 4 is about Jesus being a hugely popular teacher and miracle worker. To get a sense of what Jesus felt, have someone read **Mark 3:7–12** aloud. Then discuss the questions.

Do you think all the people who flocked to Jesus did so because, in their hearts, they were deeply interested in serving God? What other reasons might they have had for wanting to see and hear Jesus?

Jesus responded by teaching the crowd through a parable they couldn't understand—though it was actually about them! Take turns reading sections of **Mark 4:1–20** aloud. Then read the summary and discuss the remaining questions.

To summarize, Jesus was comparing his teaching to seed scattered everywhere: many people hear it, but only some are like good soil where it sinks in and grows. Other people who hear Jesus's teaching have their interest in him snatched away before it ever takes root. Still others seem devoted at first, but give up when living for Jesus becomes hard or unpopular. And others start well but get distracted by worldly lures and worries.

When people today hear about Jesus or study his teaching, how sincere are they? Are the results similar to what Jesus taught in his parable?

Think of people you know who have heard about Jesus but don't seem interested in living for him. What keeps them from embracing his word? What kind of "soil" is most common among people you know?

****

Continue to think about Jesus our teacher by reading the article aloud, taking turns at the paragraph breaks.

WHOSE STUDENT ARE YOU?

5 minutes

We have just looked at Jesus's teaching ministry, and have seen how it was a vital part of his earthly life. Even when he wasn't teaching, like when he calmed the storm at the end of chapter 4, his disciples called him *Teacher*. This was a title often given to Jesus, and Christians must embrace it. Some critics say Jesus was *only* a teacher—nothing more. As Christians, we push back and declare that he also is the Son of God (and in chapters 1 and 3 we have demons declaring it as well). Yet we must not overlook the fact that Jesus was indeed a phenomenal teacher.

But I think we can miss something that's implied by Jesus's teaching ministry: the fact that he is a teacher means you are students of someone. You see, Jesus came to this earth and spent a great deal of time teaching people. This implies we are always being taught by someone. There's a sense in which you are always in school.

Think about it this way. When you get on any media device or connect with friends that way, the images you see are teaching you something. When you listen to a certain song, that song contains a message that's teaching you. Think about the last movie you saw. Every movie has a message and that message is teaching you something. The Bible tells us our hearts are sinful, but even they are teaching us something.

You see, we are students of this world, and we are absorbing messages from the culture. We are students of our own sinful hearts, and we are learning from them each and every day. However, Jesus came to this earth to correct our thinking and teach us in the way of truth. Consider some of the differences between what a student of the world might learn and what a student of God's Word learns.

Student of the world	**Student of the Word**
"You must be the best athlete to be worthy."	"Athleticism is a gift, but your worth isn't attached to it."
"You must be the prettiest to have value."	"You may be blessed with physical beauty, but outer beauty will fade."
"You must have many followers who like what you post."	"Your value is not attached to what others think of you."
"You are your physical features."	"Your identity in Christ is more secure than your body type."

One of the greatest truths Jesus teaches is found in the parable of the sower. It is about how the Word of God may or may not bear fruit in someone's life. This is important for each of us to reflect on as we think about our own hearts.

Jesus teaches us that Satan is after us and may take the Word away when it is sown. Jesus also teaches that tribulation and persecution may take the Word away from those who at first receive it with joy. Lastly, he warns about the deceitfulness of this world choking out the Word that was sown.

It is sobering to see that there may be a season of life when the gospel seems to take root but in fact hasn't. Often, Christians are plagued with doubt about their salvation when they consider this. But Jesus is not doing this to frighten his children. Rather, being the faithful teacher that he is, Jesus is warning his children about the dangers they will encounter. He is doing this to enlighten us and sober us up to the realities of this world and the world beyond.

The point is, you are always being taught by someone or something, but there is only one true teacher.

DISCUSSION *10 minutes*

What are some of the dominant messages in our culture—the ones movies, music, and social media try to teach you? What messages would you add to the author's "Student of the world" list?

If someone were to ask you what makes Jesus better than these other teachers, what would you most want to tell them about Jesus?

FOUR KINDS OF SOIL

15 minutes

Even if you are a sincere student of Jesus, there are times you don't treat him as the supreme teacher he is. Instead, you might act like bad soil. Or perhaps you are at a point in your life where you are part of the Jesus crowd and have heard his Word, but it has not yet sunk deep into you and changed you.

Consider what kind of soil you act like. Then discuss the questions at the end of the exercise. (Be honest with yourself. Remember that God's Word starts small, like a seed, in each of us. If your growth so far seems small, that's not unusual. And if God has not yet brought you to the point of faith in Jesus, that's often a process too. It's good that you're studying the gospel.)

ACTING LIKE THE **PATH**

- ☐ I enjoy being part of the Jesus crowd, but Jesus himself doesn't seem very compelling.
- ☐ I have concerns about Jesus that keep me from committing to him.
- ☐ I may claim to follow Jesus, but I can't say I've let him teach me anything that changes how I live.

ACTING LIKE THE **ROCKY SOIL**

- ☐ I act like a Christian around other believers, but I hide that part of me when I'm with people who might disapprove.
- ☐ In the end, I have to do what's right for me. Jesus is good and all, but there's only so much I could give up for him.
- ☐ Jesus is supposed to make my life easier, and he'd better come through for me.

ACTING LIKE THE **THORNS**

- ☐ I'm really into Jesus—when I have the time for him. But life is busy, and there are priorities, you see . . .
- ☐ Honestly, most of the time I'd rather be with friends, hang out online, watch TV, play games, go shopping, wash the dog, stare at the cat, etc. Serving Jesus just isn't as much fun.
- ☐ Being part of a church is a good strategy to help me get ahead in life. I'm all for it!

ACTING LIKE THE **GOOD SOIL**

- ☐ It's hard sometimes, but I truly want Jesus to be the main teacher in my life. I'll put aside other influences if I have to.
- ☐ I can see my life start to produce fruit. Jesus's kindness to me makes me care about others, and they see his goodness too—through me.
- ☐ There's something alive in me. It's a growing godliness that makes me love others.
- ☐ I could tell you some specific things I've given up for Jesus because he's better.

Share some of your results with the group. Which of them concern or frustrate you? Which of them encourage you? Are there any you hope will change? Do you recognize some as being dangerous, but you just don't care?

Mark 4:33 sums up Jesus's teaching to the crowd this way: "With many such parables he spoke the word to them, as they were able to hear it." How does it encourage you that even though your heart is sometimes hard, Jesus keeps speaking to you patiently as you learn to really listen?

If you have an example of how Jesus has kept speaking patiently to you and you've finally listened, share that story with the group.

WRAP-UP AND PRAYER

The Holy Spirit makes your heart soft and willing to listen to Jesus's teaching. So if you want to be a better student of God's Word, thank him for giving you that desire, and ask him to make that happen in you. Pray that way now.

It's important for you to pray, especially if this lesson has made you worried that you might be in danger of being a false believer. Jesus gives us warnings so that we will turn to him in faith, and prayer is a great way to do that. If you end this lesson by praying, you will have done exactly what Jesus is urging you to do.

Before the next time you meet: Read through chapters 5 and 6 of Mark.

Lesson

3

THE COMPASSIONATE SAVIOR

BIG IDEA

Jesus is your compassionate Savior. In every way that he heals and saves you, he acts with loving concern for you.

BIBLE CONVERSATION *20 minutes*

Chapters 5 and 6 of Mark include some of Jesus's best-known and most powerful miracles. He casts out demons, brings a girl back to life, feeds a crowd, and walks on water. Mark points out that when Jesus fed the crowd "he had compassion on them" (Mark 6:34), and we can see this same compassion in the way Jesus performed the earlier miracles in chapter 5. Those will be the focus of today's study.

Have someone read **all of Mark 5 aloud** (or have a few people each read a section). Then discuss the following questions.

Look at how Jesus interacts with Jairus, a synagogue ruler, and his daughter who died. List several details that show Jesus's compassion for these people. How can you tell that Jesus was focused on those he was helping, not on his own great achievement?

Think about very powerful people you know or have heard about. What attitudes do they have toward others? What are some ways Jesus acts differently from how other powerful people tend to act?

The woman with the discharge of blood was ceremonially unclean. She would have been excluded from many social and religious settings. This means both she and the man with the demons had spiritual problems that seemed incurable, and both were outcasts. How might this explain how Jesus was caring for them when he insisted they tell their story publicly?

****

Sometimes we might imagine compassion came easily for Jesus, as if he didn't face the same human struggles we face. But the Bible says Jesus was as fully human as we are. To learn more about this, read the following article aloud, taking turns at the paragraph breaks.

Lesson

UNDERSTANDING COMPASSION

5 minutes

Sometimes it can be hard for us to believe that Jesus is truly human. I think most Christians are ready and willing to believe that Jesus is the Son of God, but we are more reluctant when it comes to his humanity. Perhaps it seems disrespectful to think of him in human terms.

Well, Scripture is clear that Jesus is the Son of God and equally clear that he is truly human. He did not stop being God when he came to earth as our Savior, but added a fully human nature to his divine nature. Mark 4:38 tells us that Jesus got tired (as humans do) and had to take a nap. At the beginning of the account of the feeding of the five thousand, we are again told how tired Jesus and his disciples were (Mark 6:31). Yet, even in his fatigue, Jesus had compassion on these people "because they were like sheep without a shepherd" (v. 35).

That said, Jesus was still really tired. He really knew what it was like to feel fatigue and need some rest and to be tempted to put his human needs ahead of his concern for others. Likewise, he too knew what it was like to be rejected—like the man possessed by the demon and the woman with the illness.

As we just discussed, both of those people felt rejection and loneliness. But rejection and loneliness are also familiar to Jesus. The beginning of chapter 6 says people misunderstood and rejected Jesus. It tells us they took offense at his teaching. We read that Jesus marveled at their unbelief. The earlier chapters in Mark tell how the disciples often misunderstood Jesus, and near the end of chapter 6 we learn that "they did not understand about the loaves, but their hearts were hardened" (Mark 6:52).

If these two chapters teach us anything, it is this: Jesus knows what it feels like to be misunderstood and rejected. When we make the mistake of forgetting that Jesus was truly human, we overlook the fact that he felt the same emotions we feel. Jesus truly knew what it was like to feel hated, lonely, outcast, bullied, and unpopular.

You do not have a Savior who doesn't understand you. In fact, you have a Savior who understands you more than anyone else you know. He understands you more than your parents and your friends. Truth be told, he understands you more than you even understand yourself.

Jesus knows you have been poisoned by sin because of the fall and you live in a fallen world, so you are going to feel the effects of sin in real and tangible ways. What brokenness are you dealing with? What sin do you still hold onto? What are you ashamed of? Know that your Savior did not keep his distance. He entered into this broken world, and he brought compassion with him—compassion for you.

DISCUSSION *10 minutes*

What have you noticed about Jesus in this lesson that you didn't notice before or that you seldom think about?

The book of Hebrews says the human sufferings and temptations Jesus faced gave him sympathy for our weaknesses and made him able to help us when we too are tempted (see Hebrews 2:18 and 4:15). Think of an example of how you are misunderstood or mistreated or how you struggle in some other way. How might it help to know that Jesus understands and has compassion on you? How might it change the way you respond in that situation?

COMPASSION RECEIVED AND GIVEN

20 minutes

When we believe in Jesus, his compassion comforts and encourages us. This lets us have compassion for others too. Jesus's way becomes our way.

Read the following statements about the compassion you receive from Jesus and the compassion you give to others. Decide how well they describe you, and then discuss the questions at the end of the exercise as a group. (NOTE: Don't worry if most (or even all!) of the statements don't seem to fit you very well at this point in your life. God gives different kinds of growth to each of us—all in his good time.)

COMPASSION RECEIVED

I am amazed and thankful that Jesus would care about a person like me and give himself for me.

- ☐ Not yet true of me
- ☐ Occasionally true of me
- ☐ Somewhat true of me
- ☐ Often true of me
- ☐ Very true of me

When the world brings me troubles or fears, I feel Jesus understands and has compassion for me.

- ☐ Not yet true of me
- ☐ Occasionally true of me
- ☐ Somewhat true of me
- ☐ Often true of me
- ☐ Very true of me

When I have spiritual problems or am tangled in sin, I feel Jesus understands and has compassion for me.

- ☐ Not yet true of me
- ☐ Occasionally true of me
- ☐ Somewhat true of me
- ☐ Often true of me
- ☐ Very true of me

Jesus's love for me makes me ready to love and obey him.

- ☐ Not yet true of me
- ☐ Occasionally true of me
- ☐ Somewhat true of me
- ☐ Often true of me
- ☐ Very true of me

COMPASSION GIVEN

I am caught up in Jesus's compassion, eager for his way to become my way too.

- ☐ Not yet true of me
- ☐ Occasionally true of me
- ☐ Somewhat true of me
- ☐ Often true of me

☐ Very true of me

God has given me a desire to help people who have troubles or fears.

☐ Not yet true of me
☐ Occasionally true of me
☐ Somewhat true of me
☐ Often true of me
☐ Very true of me

God has given me a desire to tell what Jesus has done for me to those who don't know much about him, like the man healed from the demons did.

☐ Not yet true of me
☐ Occasionally true of me
☐ Somewhat true of me
☐ Often true of me
☐ Very true of me

God has given me a desire to open up and tell what Jesus has done for me to those who already know about God, like the healed woman did.

☐ Not yet true of me
☐ Occasionally true of me
☐ Somewhat true of me
☐ Often true of me
☐ Very true of me

What do you find most interesting about your responses? Do you see any patterns or gaps in your life with God?

Where would you most like God to work in you, helping you to receive or give compassion? If you can, mention an example from your life.

WRAP-UP AND PRAYER *5 minutes*

It is God's work in you that will help you better receive and give compassion, so pray that he will help you grow in the ways you mentioned in the exercise. Remember that Jesus knows exactly how you feel, and his compassion welcomes you into his presence. Pray that this knowledge would grow in you a deeper love for him.

Before the next time you meet: Read chapters 7 and 8 of Mark.

Lesson

4

THE ONE WAY TO OVERCOME SIN

BIG IDEA

The problem you have with evil goes deeper than you think, but the finished work of Jesus solves it.

BIBLE CONVERSATION *20 minutes*

In Mark 7 and 8, Jesus pointed out two sources of evil from which he alone can save us. The first is the *selfishness and disobedience that comes from inside us.*

Jesus had just interacted with the Pharisees, who were concerned with outward spiritual cleanliness. They observed all the religious washings and only ate approved foods. Have someone read aloud what Jesus said about that in **Mark 7:14–23**. Then discuss the questions below.

Which of the evils of the heart that Jesus mentioned do you often see in your heart or in the hearts of people you know? Do any of these evils seem especially hard to overcome? Which ones, and why?

In what ways do people today, much like the Pharisees, wrongly think they can overcome their sinfulness through a few outward actions or rituals?

The second source of evil is *the lures and wrong priorities of the world outside us*. Someone please read **Mark 8:27–36** aloud. Then discuss the remaining questions.

Jesus revealed to his disciples his great purpose: that he came to suffer and die for us. When Peter tried to correct him, Jesus scolded him strongly. Jesus explained that Peter had worldly priorities rather than godly ones. What worldly priorities do you think were on Peter's mind?

Jesus taught that anyone who would follow him must die to the world. When we give up what the world offers in order to gain the life God offers, how is that a kind of death? Does it feel like death to you? Explain.

****

Replacing worldly thinking with godly thinking doesn't happen all at once. We need daily reminders of what Jesus teaches us and how he has saved us. Read about that in the article, taking turns at the paragraph breaks.

OVER AND OVER AND OVER AGAIN

5 minutes

Being a parent is one of the most rewarding and joyful experiences. But one challenging aspect to parenting, at least from my perspective, is how often I have to repeat myself to my children. *How many times have I told you not to do that? How many times have we had this discussion?* Often in my sin and selfishness, I guilt-trip and shame my own children for not remembering something I've told them.

Therefore, it is both convicting and encouraging to see the example Jesus Christ gave us. His disciplines should have known never to worry about having enough bread. Yet one time they did, and he corrected them.

> "Do you not yet perceive or understand? Are your hearts hardened? Having eyes do you not see, and having ears do you not hear? And do you not remember? When I broke the five loaves for the five thousand, how many baskets full of broken pieces did you take up?" They said to him, "Twelve." "And the seven for the four thousand, how many baskets full of broken pieces did you take up?" And they said to him, "Seven." And he said to them, "Do you not yet understand?" (Mark 8:17–21)

At this point in Mark, we are well into Jesus's earthly ministry. Jesus had been performing miracle after miracle. He even performed two very similar miracles—the feeding of the five thousand and four thousand. He had been living with the apostles on the road and having numerous conversations with them. Still, they lacked understanding.

But this was a patient and loving rebuke from Jesus. He was not shaming his disciples or giving them a guilt trip. He's encouraging them to think and be discerning. He's getting them to reflect on the signs and wonders he'd performed and getting them to draw the conclusion Mark informed us of at the beginning of his gospel: Jesus is the Son of God.

In the introduction to this study of Mark, I asked why we need a study that helps us discern the gospel in a book of the Bible that's referred to as a gospel. This is the reason. We are just like the disciples. We have eyes but do not see and ears but do not hear.

Jesus Christ was emulating his Father in how he repeated the same message over and over. I get frustrated at repeating myself, but God repeated himself from Genesis to Revelation, and we know he was slow to anger as he did this.

We also see that all this teaching has borne fruit in the disciples. As we approach the halfway point in this gospel, we read of Peter's confession that Jesus is the Christ. The readers have been told from the beginning that Jesus is the Son of God, but now those who have had a front seat to Jesus's ministry were giving this same testimony.

But notice what happens right after Peter declared Jesus to be the Christ. In the very next verses, he tried to correct Jesus about the need for Jesus to die on the cross. But Christ's sacrificial death is necessary in order for us be clean of our internal filthiness. Peter, who had gotten it so right just a few verses before, now missed the main point of Jesus's mission entirely!

We cannot be cleansed, restored, and made whole without Christ dying in our place and being raised again. And the cross and Jesus's resurrection are what give us the power to follow Jesus as he calls us to take up our own crosses. Peter, just like us, forgot that.

DISCUSSION *10 minutes*

What does God have to keep telling you over and over again because you tend to forget or ignore it?

Why is it especially important that God keeps reminding you of the core truths of the gospel—that Jesus died and rose again to save you from sin? What wrong thinking or mistakes result in your life when you fail to keep this in mind?

COME AND DIE

15 minutes

Part of what makes the gospel of Jesus good news for us is that it includes Jesus's command to lose our lives for his sake. We don't have to keep living in slavery. We can die to both the evil desires inside us and the evil lures in the world around us. We can see that Jesus is better. We can come to him, be forgiven, and be freed from sin's power over us.

One way to summarize the gospel in three points is this:

1. You are far worse than you ever imagined.
2. But Jesus loves you far more than you ever dared hope.
3. So come and die.

Read more about each point below, and note how it applies to you. Then discuss the questions at the end of the exercise.

1. You are far worse than you ever imagined.

You aren't a basically good person who slips up. As Jesus said, you have evil desires that come from your heart, causing you to sin the same way again and again. This actually is good news because it helps you be brutally honest with yourself. It means you can give up hope that you'll ever be acceptable to God on your own or that you'll be able to fix yourself by trying harder. Instead, you turn to Jesus for his forgiveness and power.

I have no hope of fixing my sin of ______________________ **except by turning to Jesus.** (If you need ideas about how to fill in the blank, look again at Jesus's list of heart sins in Mark 7:21–22.)

2. But Jesus loves you far more than you ever dared hope.

Even though Jesus triumphantly fought off every temptation he faced, he took *your* record of evil upon himself. He let himself be rejected, labeled a sinner, and killed on a cross. He suffered the shame you deserve, the curse you deserve, and the death you deserve. Now God counts you righteous, despite all your sin, because Jesus died in your place. This is cause for great joy! Not only has Jesus paid the penalty for your sin, it means you are loved to the uttermost by the best Lover who ever lived, who surely will keep you close to himself forever.

I am most amazed that Jesus would ______________________ **for me.**

3. So come and die.

All this is true for you if you come to Jesus in faith, renouncing evil and trusting him. Jesus rose from the dead; sin and death have no claim on him. And now if you are joined to him, sin and death have no lasting claim on you either. Jesus's love for you compels you, already in this life, to begin to die to both the evil inside you and the lures of the world. With God's help, you have a new way to live and a new mission. Jesus's way becomes your way.

Come and die **sounds hard, but I find it compelling because** ______ ____.

Share some of your responses with the group. What part of the gospel do you feel you need to grasp more fully or be reminded of more often? Why?

What is your new mission? And how will dying to the evil inside you and to the lures of the world free you up to live for God and others?

WRAP-UP AND PRAYER *5 minutes*

Because we are a people who forget, ask God to grow your understanding of how much Jesus loves you and how he has saved you. Ask him to help you remember it as you go through your everyday life, especially when you are tempted to have a selfish heart or to live according to the world's values.

Before the next time you meet: Read chapters 9 and 10 of Mark.

Lesson

5

THE LOVER OF THE LEAST

BIG IDEA

Jesus came to love and serve those who are the least. He calls you, as a citizen of his kingdom, to do the same.

BIBLE CONVERSATION *20 minutes*

In Mark 9 and 10, Jesus repeatedly told his disciples about his plan to suffer and die, while they had a recurring discussion (that's a nice way to put it) of their own. They argued about which of them was the greatest. Have someone read **Mark 9:30–37** aloud. Then discuss the questions below.

Based on the fact they were arguing over it, what do you think the disciples expected greatness would do for them? What benefits would it bring?

The disciples' surrounding culture was aware of who held positions of honor, and people noticed, for instance, when someone had the honor of hosting an esteemed guest. How would Jesus's teaching about the child be a challenge to the disciples' normal way of thinking?

As had happened before, Jesus needed to repeat himself when two of the disciples came to him, still seeking to be honored. Have someone read **Mark 10:35-45** aloud. Then discuss the remaining questions.

When Jesus spoke of the cup he would drink, he meant the suffering he would undergo. Why is suffering connected to greatness in Jesus's mind?

How is Jesus's own life the best possible example of the kind of greatness he was trying to teach his disciples? Think of several ways.

****

The article will continue to discuss this theme of the greatest and least in God's kingdom. Take turns reading the paragraphs aloud.

Lesson

ARTICLE

THE STRONG AND THE WEAK

5 minutes

Have you ever stopped to consider how favoritism is present in your heart? Think about the people you interact with at school or church—maybe even people in this group? Why do you want to talk to some people, but avoid talking to others? Is it favoritism?

Let's dig down further into the heart. Think about those you rarely talk to or those you avoid. Why do you avoid certain people? What is it about those you avoid that makes you avoid them? Is it because they aren't funny to you? They don't like the things you like?

Maybe they're not kind to you. That's understandable; there are a lot of reasons why we favor some people and not others. But sometimes we favor some people because they can give us something—popularity, being one. We also avoid certain people because if others see us around them, popularity can be taken away.

If you look at Mark 10:13–16, you will notice that the disciples were struggling with this very thing:

> And they were bringing children to him that he might touch them, and the disciples rebuked them. But when Jesus saw it, he was indignant and said to them, "Let the children come to me;

> do not hinder them, for to such belongs the kingdom of God. Truly, I say to you, whoever does not receive the kingdom of God like a child shall not enter it. And he took them in his arms and blessed them, laying his hands on them."

In essence, the disciples were saying, "These children aren't important enough for the Christ. Jesus is too important and too in demand for him to waste his time with these little ones." How did Jesus respond to this? He was *indignant*. What does that mean? Furious. Some commentaries tell us Jesus was so mad he was shaking.

I don't know about you, but if I saw Jesus shaking with anger I would be terrified. This is the same guy who'd been raising the dead, calming storms, and feeding thousands. The disciples would've been right to be scared.

Why was Jesus angry? He was angry because his closest followers were missing a core way Jesus's kingdom is different from the world. The men that Jesus would entrust his ministry to after his death did not care about those who were the least—but the least were the most to Jesus. Jesus has a huge heart of compassion for the weak and the outcasts, and he wanted his disciples to get this.

It is no coincidence that the account which immediately follows is about a rich young man. Let's restate that as "a wealthy, important somebody." Mark is contrasting the unimportant children with a man who had a lot of power. Jesus told his disciples to be more like the children than the rich guy. In fact, he went further and said it's the only way to enter God's kingdom: "Truly, I say to you, whoever does not receive the kingdom of God like a child shall not enter it" (Mark 10:15). Later he added, "It is easier for a camel to go through the eye of a needle than for a rich person to enter the kingdom of God" (v. 25).

The way to the kingdom of God is through Jesus Christ alone, not through power or prestige. You cannot buy the kingdom—not with money, nor by being good enough to earn it. The kingdom has already been purchased for you by the righteous life, death, and resurrection of Jesus. Coming to Jesus through humility and weakness is the path into his kingdom. Understanding that you are loved and accepted by the true King gives you more riches than this world could ever offer.

DISCUSSION *10 minutes*

The Bible says we belong to Jesus by *faith*. Faith means you believe Jesus is the Christ, the Son of God, and you receive him as your Savior from sin, entrusting your life to him instead of trusting your own goodness, abilities, and ideas. Why is Jesus's phrase like *a little child* a good way to describe this?

How does this explain why it's hard for proud people, who think they are better than others or have the means to do what they want for themselves, to have saving faith?

Think of your circle of friends. How do they rate people when they decide who to be seen with? What qualities do they look for?

How might a better understanding of how Jesus values you, in spite of your sins and unimportance, change the way you rate and value others?

Lesson

LOVING THE LEAST

15 minutes

For this exercise, break into small groups of two or three. Complete step one on your own, do step two with your small group, and then get everyone back together for step three.

STEP 1 (BY YOURSELF)

It's hard to act like a servant toward others, especially if they are people who seem less important than you or if they are people who can't pay you back—not even by being fun to be with. It takes God's work in your heart for you to be a servant to those people! This must begin with you realizing that you too are a sinner—not fun to be with, from God's perspective, but he called you to faith. Read what the Bible says about the kind of people Jesus has called to be his.

> For consider your calling, brothers: not many of you were wise according to worldly standards, not many were powerful, not many were of noble birth. But God chose what is foolish in the world to shame the wise; God chose what is weak in the world to shame the strong; God chose what is low and despised in the world, even things that are not, to bring to nothing things that are, so that no human being might boast in the presence of God. And because of him you are in Christ Jesus, who became to us wisdom from God, righteousness and sanctification and redemption. (1 Corinthians 1:26–30)

Now complete a brief sentence about how you, personally, fit the description given in that passage.

I am ____,

but in Jesus, God has given me ____________________________

____.

STEP 2 (IN GROUPS OF TWO OR THREE)

Remembering God's love for you, consider ways you can practice the kind of greatness Jesus did. Jesus left his throne in heaven and became a servant to others, giving his life for them. Think of some real-life ways to follow him.

Whom can you serve or befriend who is needy, unloved, despised, or one of the least?

What can you do to serve that person?

How can you do this in a way that doesn't end up making you look like a hero, but truly is lowly service?

STEP 3 (WITH THE WHOLE GROUP)

Share your ideas. How can you encourage one another to follow through?

WRAP-UP AND PRAYER

It's easy to hear a message and move on without taking action, so pray that God would change your heart like he changed the disciples'. Pray that he would give you a heart for the least in his kingdom. Pray that you would truly seek to serve those who are unloved or despised in your school and church.

Also pray that God would protect you from doing any of this selfishly, to earn favor with others, but that you would love others because Jesus reached out and loved you when there was nothing you had to offer.

Lesson

6

THE KING BORN TO DIE

BIG IDEA

Jesus is your Judge and King. Yet he came to this earth to die for you so that you might live and live for him.

BIBLE CONVERSATION *20 minutes*

If you think of a king, a couple of images may come to mind. One is that of a king riding triumphantly into his castle with his adoring subjects lining the way. The other is the image of a king on his throne, giving orders and sitting in judgment as cases come before him.

We are now at the point in Mark's gospel where the story slows down and goes into detail about the week leading up to Jesus's crucifixion. Listen for how Jesus takes the role of a king as you read **all of Mark 11** aloud. Then discuss the questions.

How did Jesus act like a triumphant king arriving at his palace? What are some details in Mark's account that fit the kingly image?

What were some ways Jesus acted like a king who judges, giving orders and deciding what was allowed in his kingdom?

How would you describe Jesus's attitude toward those who didn't accept his right to act like a king?

****

Jesus's kingdom brings healing and happiness, but he also is the King who came to die for his people. Read the following article aloud, taking turns at the paragraph breaks.

Lesson

ARTICLE

AN ANGRY JESUS

5 minutes

In the 2003 film *Elf* starring Will Ferrell, there's a scene where a notable children's author, Miles Finch, was angered by Buddy's incorrect assumption that he's an elf. As Miles's anger continued to grow toward Buddy, Buddy replied, "He's an angry elf."[1] Buddy seemed to be shocked that an elf got angry.

To a greater degree, some of us may read how Jesus drove people out of the temple and be shocked at his behavior. If you remember, this isn't the first time Jesus had been angry. He was also angry in the previous chapter when the disciples were keeping little children from coming to him.

What we first need to realize is that anger is not always sinful. There is a type of anger that is righteous. And, since Jesus was and is sinless, we know he was not sinning in anger. Second, we need to see that anger is often an appropriate response to life in a fallen world. As Ed Welch said, "To be human is to get angry."[2] Jesus is fully God, but he is also *fully human*. Not only was his anger sinless, it was also appropriate.

But why was Jesus angry? Even though we do read that Jesus got angry on more than one occasion, he is not frequently portrayed as angry.

---

1. *Elf*, directed by Jon Favreau (Los Angeles: New Line Cinema, 2003).
2. Edward T. Welch, *A Small Book About a Big Problem: Meditations on Anger, Patience, and Peace* (Greensboro, NC: New Growth Press, 2017), 1.

So, what happened in this section that caused him to turn tables over?

We can answer that by asking another question: What was Jesus's primary focus on earth? To do the will of his Father. Jesus said, "My food is to do the will of him who sent me and to accomplish his work" (John 4:34). Jesus loved his Father and loved worshiping him. Therefore, when Jesus saw the worship of his Father being distorted, he got angry. And this is the essence of righteous anger, when the worship of the one true God is being perverted.

But let's add another piece of the puzzle to this story. It comes from the account that immediately precedes this one, when Jesus cursed a fig tree. Why would the creator of life, Jesus Christ, kill? And, why would Mark put this story alongside the story of Jesus clearing the temple?

Well, Jesus went to eat from the fig tree because it had leaves, and this meant it looked like a place to find fruit. When it did not have any, he cursed the tree because it wasn't bearing fruit and that made it worthless. Similarly, when you see a temple you would assume worship of the Lord was happening there. But the temple was fruitless. The temple had been turned into a market of man-worship through selfish gain. It had the appearance of fruit but was fruitless like the fig tree. The fig tree was a sign that explains why Jesus was angry. Jesus loved his Father and knew his Father's house was for his worship, but it was being abused and misused by sinful men.

That said, we also see something else occurring in this story, and it is the fact that Jesus purposely drew attention to himself. Throughout most of his ministry, Jesus was careful to avoid unnecessary attention. He instructed both humans and demons to keep quiet about him. But when he came to Jerusalem, Jesus made a triumphal entry, showing how he is David's son, the king. Then he created a commotion in the temple. He was done keeping quiet about his ministry. Why? Because he came to die.

The scene in the temple sealed Jesus's fate, as "the chief priests and the scribes heard it and were seeking a way to destroy him, for they feared him, because all the crowd was astonished at his teaching" (Mark 1:18). Jesus's actions moved the hearts of those opposed to him to seek a way to kill him. While their scheme was a wicked and murderous, it played right into the will of the Father—to crush his Son that we might be saved.

This loving purpose of Jesus is the gospel. Understanding the gospel means understanding our sin. Understanding the gospel means understanding that there's a holy, righteous God who will not dwell with sinful people. Understanding the gospel means seeing that God loved us so much he sent his holy, righteous Son to die in our place. And understanding the gospel means knowing Jesus now calls us into his mission of helping other lost people find him.

DISCUSSION *10 minutes*

Think of people you know. Do you suspect that some have an outward appearance of godliness but no true heart of godliness? Why?

Why would a mere appearance of godliness make Jesus especially angry?

It seems that the more Jesus revealed his true self, the more people opposed him. How have you seen this happen today too? Which truths about Jesus make some people oppose him?

WHY ARE YOU HERE?

15 minutes

These few days in Jesus's life give you some pictures of your life with Jesus. Read the descriptions and note one or more that seem to describe your life today. Then discuss the questions at the end of the exercise.

PICTURE #1: THE FRUITLESS TREE

If you have learned much about Jesus or have grown up a Christian but have not yet put your faith in Jesus and turned away from sin, you are like the fruitless tree. You might look like someone who would serve Jesus, but it isn't happening.

- ☐ I am still unsure about Jesus because ______________________.
- ☐ I believe Jesus's claims are true, but still I resist putting my faith in him and turning away from my sin because ______________________.
- ☐ I'm good at acting like a Christian when I ____________ ______________, but I don't want my whole life to be for Jesus.
- ☐ Other fruitlessness: ______________________.

PICTURE #2: THE TABLE-TURNING KING

Jesus will not put up with a fruitless tree. If you continue to reject him, he will judge you. But if you receive him, he will bring you comfort and joy. And he will change you into the glorious, God-worshiping temple you were created to be.

- ☐ I have recently come to Jesus. I am forgiven and I feel ______________________.
- ☐ I struggle against sin and have begun to learn to trust Jesus. So far, he has helped me to ______________________.
- ☐ I am encouraged because I know that Jesus ______________________ me.
- ☐ I am learning to stay close to Jesus by praying, and by hearing and reading his Word. I need this daily because ______________________.
- ☐ Other encounter with Jesus: ______________.

PICTURE #3: THE LOVING PURPOSE

Jesus came with a purpose: to seek the lost and die for his people. When you are his disciple, he gives you a role in his mission. He calls you to participate in making disciples of all nations. You die to yourself—to serve him and love others.

- ☐ I am learning to love others by ______________.
- ☐ God has given me a desire to ______________ so that others will know Jesus and come to him.
- ☐ Jesus's love for me has softened my heart so that I am finally starting to ______________________.
- ☐ Other loving purpose: ______________.

Share some of your results with the group. Which sound most true of you? Which would you *like* to be true of you, with God's help?

Think about how these things are *connected* in your life. Answer one of the following questions:

- How has being aware of your fruitlessness helped you come to Jesus for help?
- How has your closeness to Jesus encouraged you to love others?
- When it's hard to love others, how has this made you turn back to Jesus for more comfort, new strength, and further change in your heart?

WRAP-UP AND PRAYER

If this lesson has revealed ways you desperately need God to work in your life, be sure to pray for that as a part of your closing time together.

Before the next time you meet: You will only read parts of Mark 12 together next time, so please read all of it on your own before you meet.

Lesson

7

OPPOSITION TO JESUS

BIG IDEA

Many people will oppose the gospel of Jesus Christ, and they will oppose you if you live for him.

BIBLE CONVERSATION *20 minutes*

Remember that when Jesus came to Jerusalem, he found things were not right at the temple, and he drove out those who did business there. The religious leaders, whom God had made caretakers of the temple, challenged Jesus's authority to do this and plotted to destroy him. Chapter 12 of Mark picks up with Jesus challenging the religious leaders right back. He told a parable that's about them: how they were evil caretakers who would not listen to God's prophets and now wanted to kill the Son of God.

Have someone read **Mark 12:1–12** aloud. Then discuss the following questions.

The fact that Jesus would tell this parable in this situation shows his character. What kind of person does he prove to be? How can you see both his strength and his compassion?

After Jesus told the parable against them, the religious leaders tried to trap Jesus with a series of questions, but he answered without falling for their traps. Then he spoke against them again. Read **Mark 12:38–44**, and discuss the remaining questions.

According to this passage, how are the heart-level motives of a person who opposes Jesus different from those of one who is devoted to God? List several ways.

How do you think we can tell the difference between a person who might outwardly look appealing and worth following and perhaps even religious, and one who is truly devoted to God?

****

Let's consider this theme more in the article that follows. Take turns reading it aloud.

Lesson

ARTICLE

THE ENCOURAGEMENT OF OPPOSITION

5 minutes

I remember walking down the street of a very large city that was home to an NFL team. It was freezing so I was wearing a sock hat, and I didn't give too much thought to the fact that my sock hat had the emblem of this particular city's NFL rival. Well, I didn't get too far before I received some annoying looks from strangers. I even had a couple of guys say some words that cannot be repeated in this study. Although it wasn't too shocking to hear their disdain, it was a little unnerving to hear complete strangers display hatred toward someone they didn't even know.

Having other people like us can be an idol, but there's also a biblical truth to consider here. Every human was created in the likeness of God, and dwelling in perfect unity together is an implication of living as an image bearer. Therefore, when someone doesn't like us—hates us, even—this goes against our creational desire to dwell with fellow humans in peace and harmony.

What does all of this have to do with the gospel? Well, the Bible tells us that we will be hated by others because of our belief in Jesus Christ. Surveying the Scriptures, we find that opposition to God's way and God's people is a clear theme.

Looking in chapter 12, we see the Sadducees opposing Jesus (vv. 18–27). Their question wasn't so much about the resurrection as it was about trying to trip Jesus up and make him look foolish.

However, Jesus is perfectly loving and gracious even to those who oppose him. He came to die for sinners and offers new life to everyone who will believe—even those who hate him. Those of us who believe in Jesus as our Savior need to realize that we once were people who opposed the message of the gospel (Titus 3:3).

While the language of "enemies" and "opposition" may sound strong to some, it's a truth we must understand as Christians. You see, we weren't just a "little bad" or "slightly off" in our thoughts and attitudes toward Christ. We were running in the other direction, content in our rebellion, yet God reached out and saved us by his baffling grace. You see, the deeper we grasp our opposition and rebellion, the deeper we grasp the grace that was lavished upon us.

Therefore, the encouragement of opposition can be seen in our own lives. That is, we can reflect upon God's love manifested in our own hearts of opposition, and by grace extend the same favor to others who oppose us. However, there is another aspect of encouragement we can glean from opposition.

At first glance, this might not seem too encouraging, but hear me out. You see, it may shock, discourage, and hurt when we feel opposition and hatred from others as we attempt to share the love of Christ with them. As I said, some of this is rooted in the creational truth of unity. But encouragement can come from the fact that the Bible promises us that we will be opposed.

Like I said, this might seem like a head-scratching "encouragement," but the encouragement lies in the fact that God, in his fatherly care, has prepared us for this opposition—we shouldn't be caught off guard. Plus, opposition and hatred can often move us to despair—even doubt—what it is we claim to believe. However, God's fatherly preparation for opposition in the Christian life can give us certainty and confidence to assert the gospel, even in the face of opposition.

So, even though it may seem like a "discouraging encouragement," we can be prepared for it. Expect it. Live with it. And give thanks to God that his grace entered in to our initial opposition to him.

DISCUSSION *10 minutes*

Have you ever tried to share the gospel with someone? Why or why not? If so, how did they receive it?

Does the reality of opposition to the Christian life encourage or discourage you? What are some other ways it can be both encouraging and discouraging?

What do you think the author meant by our creational desire to be liked? Put this in your own words.

What could opposition to the gospel look like in your everyday life? At your school? On your sports team? In other areas? Does it seem that many of your friends oppose the gospel?

OPPOSING MESSAGES

15 minutes

Since Jesus faced opposition, you can expect to as well. You can also learn how to face opposition by looking at how Jesus faced it. Hebrews 12:3 says, "Consider him who endured from sinners such hostility against himself, so that you may not grow weary or fainthearted."

Read the descriptions of Jesus and consider how they might apply to you. Then discuss the questions at the end of the exercise.

JESUS: Jesus was brave. He spoke the truth that needed to be said and did not hold back. He did this even when people were plotting to kill him for it.

YOU: The fear of opposition or of being dismissed might keep you from speaking up when you should. Or it might keep you from saying no to sin or from showing kindness to needy people when it's not popular.

- ☐ I want to be brave enough to say ________________.
- ☐ I want the courage to live openly for Jesus even when ____________________________.
- ☐ I don't want ____________________________ to keep me from being kind to others.
- ☐ Other courage: ________________________.

JESUS: Jesus was patient and caring. He gave his opponents many opportunities to listen to him and change their ways, and he spoke to them honestly about their need and what he offered.

YOU: A lack of concern for others might be another reason you hide your faith, ignore the needy, or don't say no to sin. Or you might dream of your enemies' downfall more than you hope for their salvation.

- ☐ I want to care enough to talk about ______________________ when it might be helpful.
- ☐ I think I can make a positive difference by ______________________.
- ☐ I can love my enemies by ________________, and can pray for those who persecute me (Matthew 5:44).
- ☐ Other caring: ______________________.

JESUS: Jesus expected opposition, yet he did not despair. He had confidence that God was accomplishing great things even when many people rejected him.

YOU: A feeling that it won't really make any difference might keep you from sharing about Jesus or trying to help others.

- ☐ I want to become confident that God can use me to ______________________.
- ☐ I want to learn that God is in charge of ______________________ even though I can't seem to make any headway with it/them.
- ☐ Other confidence: ______________________.

Share some of your thoughts with the group. Try to include specific examples.

Now consider and discuss this: Jesus's situation was unique. He had the authority to overturn tables and scold Bible teachers. But *you* are not the Son of God, and your opponents might not be plotting to kill you. So, how do you deal bravely with opposition while still showing appropriate, godly respect for others?

WRAP-UP AND PRAYER

Pray that you would have the four characteristics discussed in the exercise—boldness, love, confidence, and respectful humility—toward those who may oppose you as you live for Jesus. Pray also for a heart that desires to speak the truth about Jesus to others.

Lesson

8

THE COMING OF THE KINGDOM

BIG IDEA

Because Jesus's return is approaching and times are dangerous until then, his followers must remain awake.

BIBLE CONVERSATION *20 minutes*

After warning his disciples about the religious leaders in Mark 12, Jesus warns about the future in chapter 13. Some of what he predicted happened about forty years later, when the Romans tore apart the temple, and other parts may have been happening for a long time now. But still other events Jesus revealed seem to have not happened yet and are in our future. Take turns reading **all of chapter 13** aloud. Then discuss the questions.

Jesus's picture of the future shows what the world looks like when people try to be their own gods instead of following him. List several ways such a future is bleak for everyone.

Why did Jesus decide to tell that some parts of the future will be dangerous? What things does he want believers to do?

In what ways is the future also full of hope for believers, according to Jesus?

Why do you think Jesus also told about the hopeful parts of our future?

****

Jesus gives us this picture of the future to prepare us for the days ahead. He also gives us an important piece of advice, which we will look at in the article. Take turns reading it aloud.

PULLING AN ALL-NIGHTER FOR JESUS

5 minutes

I don't know about you, but I'm tired—a lot! I have trouble falling asleep. I often wake up in the middle of the night because I have five young children who don't always sleep through the night. I try to exercise, so that also makes me tired. I also try to wake up early (not all the time) to have devotional time with the Lord. All of this makes me tired.

But I'm also tired because of the sin in my heart. My sin makes me worry; it creates anxieties about everything. As I've grown older, I've grown to see my sin more. This also makes me exhausted.

Therefore, I have external factors and internal factors that make me tired. But I worship a Savior who knew what it was like to be tired. Much of the gospel of Mark has given us pictures of Jesus's humanity, so we can understand that Jesus was familiar with our weaknesses and struggles. Jesus understood the fatigue we often feel, and he knows falling asleep is going to be a temptation for us.

In Mark 13:32–37, Jesus said "stay awake" three times and "keep awake" once. Now, he wasn't simply talking about pulling an all-nighter and just staying up to party or binge-watch. Jesus was pointing his disciples back to what he previously said about the destruction to come.

Throughout this chapter Jesus gave us a glimpse of the future. And then, because he's a great teacher, he went on to explain this future by giving a picture of this reality. Jesus said it is like a master going on a journey who gives his servants work to do and commands the doorkeeper to stay awake. Those servants wouldn't want to be found sleeping if the master returns suddenly.

In essence, Jesus was saying he's leaving for a trip, but he's coming back. And while he is gone on this trip, his servants will be tempted to fall asleep, which is a euphemism for turning away from Christ. Jesus was not saying that his true followers can fall away from the faith, but he was saying that many who appeared to be servants will turn away because of this opposition or the cares of the world. Think back to the parable of the sower in Mark 4.

Jesus commands us to remain awake so we will be on guard and be wise about false teachers who will tempt us to "fall asleep." Twice in this section, Jesus gave us warnings. First, he told us these false teachers will lead many astray (Mark 13:5–6), making it vital we remain awake so we too aren't led astray. He then discussed the miracles and wonders these false teachers would perform (vv. 21–23). He went so far as to say these false teachers would be so convincing that even the elect, were it not for God's constraining grace, would be led astray.

If all this talk of the future does not sober or even frighten you, you aren't paying attention. But Jesus said these things to prepare and guard his children, and amid all the bleakness he also gave us hope. At the end, his people "will see the Son of Man coming in clouds with great power and glory. And then he will send out the angels and gather his elect from the four winds, from the ends of the earth to the ends of heaven" (vv. 26–27). Despite the opposition, Jesus is still in charge. He is coming back. He is going to take care of you and all of his children.

DISCUSSION *10 minutes*

Which of the troubles Jesus warned about feels like the biggest danger to you, one that would threaten to make you fall away from faith? Why?

Is there a promise Jesus has made or something he has done for you that would help you stay faithful if you faced these threats? What is it, and how would it help you?

KEEPING A WATCHFUL EYE

15 minutes

Consider some practical ways you can "stay awake" and be well-prepared when scary or tempting times come in life. The chart below shows some ways you might live as either a wakeful person or a sleepy one. Read through it and note some items that apply to you. Then discuss the questions at the end of the exercise.

Living like a WAKEFUL person	**Living like a SLEEPY person**
I spend time reading the Bible. It reminds me of God's love for me and keeps me focused on his kingdom and his way of living—so I need it!	The Bible is okay, I guess. I have a Bible for group studies. I don't make much time for it otherwise.
I also *hear* the Word of God preached, in church, where I'm encouraged weekly by God's people and our worship together. It keeps me alert to the things of God.	I might enjoy church, but I'm not sure it's a spiritual necessity. I probably ought to be there when I can, if it works into my schedule.

I'm honest with other believers about my sins and temptations. Bringing my sin out into the open helps me keep fighting it.

I'm more comfortable hiding my sin and fighting it on my own. Actually, much of the time I just give in to sin without fighting it at all.

I confess to God, too, who's my partner in the fight against sin. Confession lets me enjoy God's forgiveness anew every day and keeps me longing for better days ahead with him.

If I pray at all, I prefer to avoid the uncomfortable topic of my sin. That's just too much negativity!

I am on the lookout for opportunities to love and help others like Jesus has loved and helped me.

When I see others in need, I hope someone else will help them so I don't have to.

I pay attention to Jesus's kingdom. Watching how God is at work throughout the world, bringing people to salvation, reminds me what a great mission I have as his child.

I mostly just pay attention to myself and how God might help me.

I'm constantly finding reasons to pray to my Father. I need his help for everything I do.

Prayer is boring and feels unnecessary. I prefer to solve my own problems. If I do something for God, I'd rather do it to impress him than do it *with* him.

I pray often. This means I live my life alongside my Father, close to him. No part of my life is hidden from him.	I feel distant from God, like he could come back and I'd be one of the people still hiding from him.
I am aware that I will die and have to account for my time in this world. I have limited days to live for God here. Remembering this gives me a heart of wisdom (Psalm 90:12).	I bounce along as if I will live forever. There's plenty of time left in my life for me to repent of my sin and get work done for God. Maybe that will just happen naturally someday.
I know that life here is brief and hard, but the next world is glorious and eternal. I am focused on laying up for myself treasures in heaven that will never be lost (Matthew 6:20).	The treasures and glories of earth are easier to see and can be mine now. Obviously, they capture most of my attention.

In what ways are you wakeful, and in what ways are you sleepy? Where would you like to become more wakeful?

If you can, share an example of a specific incident in your life that showed either a wakeful or sleepy attitude toward God.

How might it help you remain wakeful if you remember the vision of Jesus returning in clouds with great power and glory to gather his people from the ends of the earth? If you can, give an example from your life.

WRAP-UP AND PRAYER *5 minutes*

Being wakeful is not something you do on your own as a performance for God, but rather something to do with him as he helps you. So end your time together by praying for wakefulness.

- Ask God to give you awareness of his goodness to you and the approach of his glorious return.
- Pray that you will be sobered by the dangers that threaten you so that you will remain watchful.
- Pray for an urgency in your life to fight sin, work for God's kingdom, and tell others about Jesus.
- Ask that God would help you develop faithful habits of reading and listening to his Word, praying, confessing sin, and meeting with other believers.

Lesson

9

LOVING THE UNLOVABLE

BIG IDEA

Even amid your denial and betrayal, Jesus remains faithful to love you.

BIBLE CONVERSATION *20 minutes*

Mark 14 begins two days before Jesus's death on the cross. If ever Jesus needed faithful friends, it was during these days. But these were dangerous days not only for him but also for any disciples who might be caught with him. Have someone read **Mark 14:1–11** aloud. Then discuss the question.

The guests at the meal included Jesus's disciples (see Matthew 26:8). How might you contrast their attitude toward Jesus with the woman's attitude? Think of several differences.

The scene now moves ahead to the evening before Jesus was arrested. Read **Mark 14:12–38**. Then discuss the questions.

It turns out that after Jesus was beaten, mocked, and condemned to die, Peter did get scared and denied knowing Jesus. How would this add to the hurt Jesus was already experiencing?

Even though Peter and the other disciples were cold toward Jesus and abandoned him, how did Jesus keep loving them? List several ways this passage shows he cared for them.

****

The article has more thoughts on Jesus's suffering and his relationship with his disciples. Read it aloud, taking turns at the paragraph breaks.

DENYING JESUS

5 minutes

When we talk about the suffering of Jesus, I think most of our minds go to the cross, and rightly so. The suffering Jesus endured there is truly beyond our finite minds. It was bloody and graphic—exceedingly wicked and horrible.

That said, we should not minimize the constant suffering Jesus endured from the moment of his birth. He was the inventor of legs, yet he had to learn how to walk. He had infinite strength, yet needed rest. He was fulfilled in every sense of the word, yet needed food to survive. He had perfect fellowship with God the Father and God the Holy Spirit, but dwelt with a group of people who fought over who was the greatest and denied their true friend. That is suffering.

When we read of Jesus being anointed at Bethany, we might not see how the commotion this caused was a denial, but it was. Jesus is the true King and lover of the least, yet those present at this meal denied it. The woman was well aware of Jesus's worth and spent great wealth out of appreciation for who Christ was and is. Yet those who witnessed it scolded her and became furious.

Jesus defended the woman, but he was also defending who he is. Yes, he was pointing to his death—"you will not always have me" (v. 7)—but he was also telling them that he was the one the Law and the Prophets predicted. He was the one headed to the cross to endure God's wrath. She had anointed Jesus for his burial, but their indignance at her act was denying that. They were focused on earthly wealth and missed the eternal wealth in their presence.

This means Jesus was suffering on a relational level. Those around him were going to scatter rather than stand by him. One would betray him, and another would deny knowing him. And all of them were missing the point: they did not see who he was and what he was headed to do. But Jesus knew what was coming.

The Lord's Supper is familiar to most of us. But what do you think was going through our Savior's mind as he instituted it that night. He said, "Take; this is my body." He knew, as he broke the bread, that his body was going to be broken—literally. When he said, "This is my blood," he knew his blood was about to be poured out. As the disciples drank the cup, he knew he would drink the cup of God's wrath—a cup we could not drink and a cup our minds cannot grasp (vv. 22–25).

You see, Jesus's suffering began prior to the cross. He knew the wrath and pain that was coming. Yet he willingly suffered for those who would deny him.

Answer this question for yourself: Have you ever denied Jesus? Just think about that for a moment. Here's the answer: you have. You have denied and betrayed the perfect Son of God. You may want to push back on that or deny the fact that you've denied Jesus, but it's true. You have. And still he died for you.

DISCUSSION *10 minutes*

What do you think the author means when he insists that you have denied Jesus?

How have you been like the guests at the feast in Bethany, failing to see Jesus's worth or appreciate all he's done for you?

How have you been like Peter, who got scared and didn't want anyone to know he was with Jesus?

Lesson

THE SELFISHNESS OF SIN

15 minutes

One thing sin does is turn you inward. It makes you self-focused: you think about how your sin annoys you because it makes *you* feel guilty or stressed, or you fear being exposed because it would embarrass *you*.

But as with Peter's denial of Jesus, your sin hurts others. It often damages your relationships, and it always is rebellion against the God who loves you. It's good for you to be aware of how your sin is hurtful; it helps you take it seriously.

You will begin this exercise by reflecting on ways your sin hurts others and offends God, using the questions below. Take some time in personal reflection and prayer as you work through steps one, two, and three. Then discuss the questions at the end of the exercise with the group.

STEP 1: REFLECT ON HOW YOU HAVE HURT OTHERS

How has your sin hurt others or damaged your relationships? It may be

- *something you have done* that was selfish, rather than loving your neighbor as you love yourself—something hurtful, unfaithful, greedy, avoiding opportunities to serve, etc.,

- *something you have said* that hurt or disrespected your parents, teachers, friends, siblings, or others. It could be something you said to them, or something said behind their backs or on social media, or
- *something you have thought* about your friends, parents, teachers, the opposite sex, or others, that is unfair or unkind.

Reflect for a moment on how you have hurt others, and confess this sin to God.

STEP 2: REFLECT ON HOW YOU HAVE REBELLED AGAINST GOD

When King David committed murder and adultery, he realized these were not just sins against others but were first of all sins against God. He prayed to God, "Against you, you only, have I sinned and done what is evil in your sight" (Psalm 51:4).

Reflect for a moment on how your sin against others shows you are unwilling to trust and obey God. Confess this to God.

STEP 3: REFLECT ON HOW YOU HAVE DENIED JESUS

How have you denied your Savior? It may be

- a way you disobeyed God even though you claim to be a Christian,
- a way you failed to see or appreciate Jesus's worth and his love for you, or
- a way you acted like you weren't a believer (or even said it directly) because you were afraid for others to know.

Reflect for a moment on how you have denied Jesus, and confess your sin to God.

STEP 4: REFLECT ON HOW FAITHFULLY JESUS HAS LOVED YOU

Yes, you have been unfaithful to Jesus. But 2 Timothy 2:13 says, "If we are faithless, he remains faithful—for he cannot deny himself." Jesus never fails to be the loving person he is! Consider some of the blessings mentioned so far in the book of Mark that Jesus faithfully gives to unfaithful people like you. Which of them are most encouraging to you?

- ☐ Jesus gives me the Spirit to teach me holiness. "He will baptize you with the Holy Spirit" (Mark 1:8).
- ☐ Jesus calls me to himself even though I am a sinner. "I came not to call the righteous, but sinners" (Mark 2:17).
- ☐ Jesus forgives my sin. "All sins will be forgiven the children of man" (Mark 3:28).
- ☐ Jesus welcomes me into his family. "Whoever does the will of God, he is my brother and sister and mother" (Mark 3:35).
- ☐ Jesus shares the deep truths of God with me. "To you has been given the secret of the kingdom of God" (Mark 4:11).
- ☐ Jesus came to serve and give his life for me. "For even the Son of Man came not to be served but to serve, and to give his life as a ransom for many" (Mark 10:45).
- ☐ Jesus will gather me to be with him forever. "He will send out the angels and gather his elect" (Mark 13:27).
- ☐ Jesus bled for me. "This is my blood of the covenant, which is poured out for many" (Mark 14:24).
- ☐ Jesus is waiting to feast with me in glory. "I will not drink again of the fruit of the vine until that day when I drink it new in the kingdom of God" (Mark 14:25).

STEP 5: DISCUSS WITH THE GROUP

If you are comfortable doing so, share some of your reflections that might be helpful and appropriate.

Think of the ways Jesus remains faithful to you. Which do you find most encouraging, and why? How do they help you remain more faithful to him?

WRAP-UP AND PRAYER

Remember that to make progress spiritually, you need God's help—so you need to pray. With that in mind, make good use of this time by praying.

Pray that you would be humbled by your sin, impacted by Jesus's suffering, and encouraged by his faithfulness to you. Pray that God would deepen your love for this faithful Savior.

Lesson

10

THE SUFFERING SERVANT

BIG IDEA

If you are God's child, Jesus loved you enough to suffer and die for you. And you will suffer for him too.

BIBLE CONVERSATION *20 minutes*

Beginning midway through Mark 14, Jesus's suffering becomes a major theme. Take turns reading **Mark 14:32–72** aloud. Then discuss the questions below.

What are some ways Jesus suffered physically?

How did Jesus also suffer emotionally?

How was Jesus's suffering hurtful for him personally? Consider the behavior of both his enemies and his closest disciples.

The prospect of suffering might make us think we have an understandable excuse to obey God less rigorously. How is Jesus's approach to suffering different?

****

Now read more about how Jesus showed his love by suffering. Take turns reading through the article aloud.

WAITING IS THE HARDEST PART

5 minutes

One of the greatest directors in cinematic history is Steven Spielberg. And one of his greatest tools is his ability to create tension through anticipation. Think about the distant thud shaking a cup of water as the mighty T. rex begins to approach in *Jurassic Park*. Your heart begins to race because you know something very large is coming.

Spielberg's greatest tension of all—possibly in any movie ever—comes from the apex predator of the deep. The great white shark in *Jaws* forever changed the summer movie season and our thoughts about swimming in the open ocean. Spielberg owes a great deal of thanks to the musical composer, John Williams, and those two notes that incite fear in most humans: duh-dunt.

Anticipation can be exciting, but it can also be terrifying. It's exciting to anticipate a trip or birthday. It's horrifying, at times, to anticipate our own death. While we all face the sobering reality of death, Jesus's anticipation of it was heightened because he knew it was coming. We have the luxury of not knowing how or when we will go. Jesus knew the day, the hour, and the events leading up to it. That's excruciating.

After praying in Gethsemane, Jesus heard the crowd coming. Although Mark does not tell us much about Jesus's thoughts, Jesus clearly knew his earthly mission would lead to the cross, so it's safe to say he had reflected on this moment prior to it coming. The anticipation grew as he heard the footsteps, the armor clanking together, the light from the torches approaching. This was the moment Jesus came for. This was the moment he had predicted. Surely, this was the moment he had been thinking of countless times before.

The anticipation of this event is an added layer of suffering for Christ. Try to consider that he knew this was coming. For example, what if you were told the day and hour you were going to die? Every day leading up to that day would create more tension and sorrow and fear. Jesus's prayer in Gethsemane illustrates the distress.

Yet even in the midst of all the pain and affliction Christ was experiencing, he was focused on his task. Jesus said, "Have you come out as against a robber, with swords and clubs to capture me? Day after day I was with you in the temple teaching, and you did not seize me. *But let the Scriptures be fulfilled*" (Mark 14:48–49, emphasis mine).

Through all the distress, Jesus was laser-focused on his Father's words coming to completion. In essence he was saying, "You guys had plenty of opportunities to do this, but you waited until now. And the real reason you waited is because this was exactly how my Father wanted this to happen. Even through your wickedness, you are only accomplishing what my Father wanted you to do."

DISCUSSION *10 minutes*

What insights about Jesus's suffering seem new to you? How does Mark's reporting help you see the greatness of Jesus's love for you in new ways?

Describe a situation in your life when obeying God might involve some hardship or suffering. Do you think the anticipation of suffering would make it even harder to obey, or would it be easier to obey if you knew in advance the hardships were coming? Explain why.

SUFFERING SERVANTS

15 minutes

We have seen how Jesus is the ultimate suffering servant. But as his followers, we too are called to suffer for the sake of the gospel. In fact, whenever we hide our faith or fail to live for Jesus, it often is because we are not willing to suffer or be mistreated—as happened with Peter.

This exercise has two questions about suffering for Jesus, each with several suggested answers. Note some answers that apply to you. Then discuss the additional questions at the end of the exercise. (NOTE: God puts each of us in different situations, so try to avoid comparing your experience with what has happened to others.)

QUESTION 1: WHAT HAVE YOU GIVEN UP FOR JESUS?

Back in Mark 10:29, Jesus said his followers might give up "house or brothers or sisters or mother or father or children or lands" for his sake. Following Jesus includes sacrifice. What have you given up?

SIN

- ☐ I have given up a sinful activity I know displeased God.
  Explain: ______________________________

☐ I fear how my life will change or might seem less fun if I give up my sin.

Explain: ______________________________

SELFISHNESS

☐ I have given up a selfish way of living that kept me from loving others well.

Explain: ______________________________

☐ I fear the sacrifices involved in being selfless.

Explain: ______________________________

SELF-TRUST

☐ I have given up a way of trusting myself so I can trust God instead.

Explain: ______________________________

☐ I fear trusting God. Who knows what he might decide for me?

Explain: ______________________________

COMFORTS

☐ I have given up something comfortable, fun, or valuable in order to serve others.

Explain: ______________________________

☐ I fear missing out on my favorite comforts and enjoyments.

Explain: ______________________________

REPUTATION

☐ I have given up my reputation with family, school, church, friends, team, etc.

Explain: ______________________________

☐ I fear how serving Jesus, or doing it openly, might affect my reputation.

Explain: ______________________________

RIGHTEOUS APPEARANCES

☐ I have confessed a sin to others even though I wasn't forced into it.

Explain: ______________________________

☐ I fear confessing sin if it won't let me keep up good appearances.

Explain: ______________________________

QUESTION 2: HOW HAVE YOU BEEN MISTREATED BECAUSE OF JESUS?

The Bible says, "All who desire to live a godly life in Christ Jesus will be persecuted" (2 Timothy 3:12). Not all believers are threatened with beatings or death, such as Peter probably feared. But that could happen to you, or you might face some other mistreatment.

EXCLUSION

☐ Others have excluded me because of my choices to follow Jesus.

Explain: ______________________________

☐ I fear being left out if I openly obey Jesus.

Explain: ______________________________

STRESS

☐ I suffer difficult relationships because others don't understand my faith.

Explain: ______________________________

☐ I fear the stress on my relationships if I'm open about my faith.

Explain: ______________________________

CRITICISM

☐ I have been teased or criticized because of Jesus.

Explain: ______________________________

☐ I fear being teased or criticized if I live for Jesus.

Explain: ______________________________

LOSS

☐ I have had things taken from me or have been kept out of an activity or a friendship or haven't received honor because of Jesus.

Explain: ______________________________

☐ I fear loss or not being able to participate or not staying on top.

Explain: ______________________________

Share some of your results with the group.

How does Jesus's example help you be willing to suffer and sacrifice?

What is one way Jesus has loved you or one promise he gives you that helps you be willing to suffer and sacrifice? Explain why it helps.

WRAP-UP AND PRAYER *5 minutes*

Sometimes the exercises in this book may remind you how much you fall short in serving Jesus. Rather than feel crushed, take your failures to God. If you have faith in Jesus, remember these three things:

1. **You are counted righteous.** God will not judge you by how well you obey. Instead, he credits you with the perfect obedience of Jesus, which we've seen in this lesson. "We have been justified by faith" (Romans 5:1).

2. **You are forgiven.** God is not holding a grudge against you. He surely forgives you when you confess your wrongs. "If we confess our sins, he is faithful and just to forgive us our sins" (1 John 1:9).

3. **You have help.** Jesus is on your side. Ask him to make you fruitful. "Whoever abides in me, and I in him, he it is that bears much fruit" (John 15:5).

Wrap up your time together by thanking God for these things and by asking for his forgiveness and help.

Lesson

11

THE FORSAKEN SON

BIG IDEA

Jesus secured your redemption by paying the penalty for your sin.

BIBLE CONVERSATION *20 minutes*

Mark's gospel reaches its high point as Jesus headed to the cross, beginning with him being sent to the Roman governor Pilate who had the authority to order his crucifixion. Have someone read **Mark 15:1–15** aloud. Then discuss the question below.

How does Mark's account show that Jesus was an innocent man who in no way deserved to die and that a great injustice was taking place? List several details that show this.

Now take turns reading **Mark 15:16–39** aloud. Then discuss the remaining questions.

Our sin means we not only deserve punishment, but we also deserve shame and to be cursed and forsaken by God. What are several ways Jesus suffered shame as part of his death?

How does Mark's account also show that Jesus's death represents being cursed and forsaken by God?

Why, do you think, did the Roman centurion in charge of the crucifixion reach the conclusion that Jesus was the Son of God? Does the centurion's witness help to convince you as well? Explain.

****

To think more deeply about this, take turns reading the following article aloud.

Lesson

11

ARTICLE

AND NOW, THE MOMENT WE'VE ALL BEEN WAITING FOR

5 minutes

As you have probably realized from this study, I'm a bit of a movie fan. I enjoy going to the movies, and much of my childhood was spent in front of the silver screen. I love going to the movies, except . . . when I don't.

As you know, we all have great experiences at the movies, but we also have bad ones. There are movies we watch and then rewatch. Movies we cannot wait to talk about. Movies that create an exciting memory with friends. And then there are movies we watch and think, *I'm never watching this again. What a waste of time.* There are those movies we may even walk out on because they're terrible in every sense of the word.

Sometimes movies are ruined because of the hype. Perhaps a movie was so hyped and talked about so much, you couldn't wait to see it. Then, when the time finally came, it just didn't live up to the hype.

When we get to the story of Jesus Christ dying on the cross, it's the most hyped story in the history of the world. God showed a preview for it way back in the garden of Eden, when he said the offspring of a woman would crush the evil serpent's head (Genesis 3:15). Every book in the

Old Testament builds up to this one moment at the cross, and all the events in the New Testament point us to it.

Even the last event before Jesus was handed over to be crucified—the release of Barabbas—showed how Jesus is the innocent one whose death allows the guilty to go free. This is absurd, but it's the gospel. This most violent act reconciles us to God and creates peace. It changes murderers like you and me into sons and daughters of the King.

Ultimately, every story in literature, television, movies, and music contains elements of this one story in the Bible. It's the most hyped-up story, and yet it's the only one that truly lives up to the hype. Don't believe me? Let's think a little bit more.

The cross is the only reason you can have joy. It's the only reason you can have friends. It's the only reason you can have hope in this fallen world. You can have joy because you know your sins were payed for. You can have friends because the cross reconciled you to God and taught you how to love and forgive others. You can have hope in this world because you know redemption has been accomplished and future restoration is coming.

The cross takes all your embarrassing, shame-inducing, filthy acts and pays for them. This includes the things you do which displease God, plus the things you don't do that God commands you to do. Jesus has paid for them all, because he never displeased God and always did what God commanded.

However, Jesus not only paid for your sins, but he also took the guilt and shame that accompanies your sin and nailed them to the cross. Therefore, when you mess up and feel guilty for it, you can stop feeling guilty. Of course, this is easier said than done. But you can start believing, knowing that Satan wants you to remain in your guilt but Jesus killed your guilt—so boast in that!

Our sin caused every bit of Christ's suffering, but it was the Father's will to crush his Son (Isaiah 53:10). Yes, there was a sense in which our sin nailed Jesus Christ to the cross. Our sin had to be paid for. Our sin incited the righteous fury and wrath of God. But there's also a sense in which love sent Jesus to the cross.

In Jesus Christ, you are loved and accepted by God. And the Scriptures tell us that God reached out to you and loved you when there was nothing in you that made you worthy—got that? While you were still a sinner, Christ died for you (Romans 5:8). Glory in the beauty of the cross.

DISCUSSION *10 minutes*

What are some ways the cross is under-hyped in our culture? Are most people comfortable thinking about the cross, or do they prefer not to? Why is that?

How much do you think about the cross, and what are your reasons for thinking about it or preferring not to?

Which of the things that Jesus did for you on the cross are you quick to think about, and which parts do you tend to put out of your mind? Why?

LIVING OUT THE GOSPEL

15 minutes

In this lifetime, none of us fully grasp the tremendous power of the cross. Often, we may have whole areas of the Christian life in which we barely sense all Jesus has done for us by his death and resurrection. And so this good news—the gospel—fails to power our lives.

Read the following explanations of the gospel's power in four areas of the Christian life. Then rate yourself: Do you feel the cross has a small impact or a big (but still growing!) impact on your life in that area, or is it somewhere in between? When you finish, discuss the questions at the end of the exercise.

AREA 1: JUSTIFYING POWER

If you have faith in Jesus, his death on the cross means he has paid the full price for your sin. He has taken your guilt. He has taken your shame. He has taken the curse you deserve. He has died the death you deserve. And in return, God counts you as having the righteous record Jesus earned by his perfect life. "For our sake he made him to be sin who knew no sin, so that in him we might become the righteousness of God" (2 Corinthians 5:21).

A big appreciation for the **justifying power** of the cross in your life will mean:

- You are no longer hounded by fear that God may be planning to punish you.
- You walk around with confidence that God loves you and will use you, rather than living with guilt and shame.
- You don't feel a need to hide your sin and you are open to correction because your joy and security is not based on your own reputation.
- You love others and make amends because you want to, not out of fear that you need to prove your devotion to God.
- You don't mind taking a hard look at God's law and your sin because you aren't scared to see what a big sinner you still are.
- You are thankful to God.

In my life, the **justifying power** of the cross feels . . .

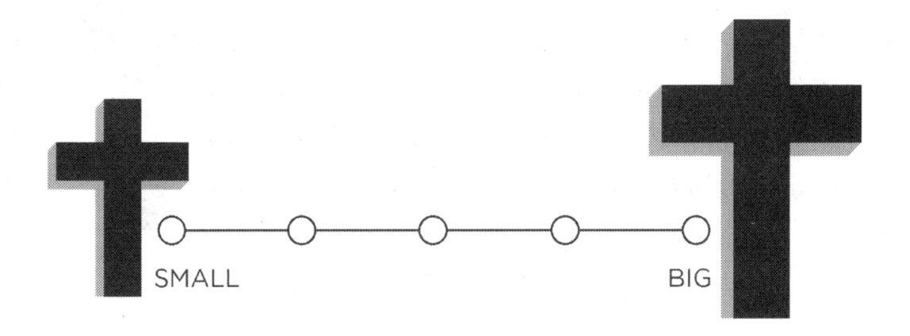

AREA 2: CHILD-OF-GOD POWER

On the cross, Jesus became the forsaken one so that, by faith in him, you could become a child of God. You are an heir to every good gift from your Father. You have his love, his attention, his daily care, his constant provision, and his wise discipline. "See what kind of love the Father has given to us, that we should be called children of God; and so we are" (1 John 3:1).

A big appreciation for the **child-of-God power** of the cross in your life will mean:

- You are not anxious, even in hard times, knowing that your Father is working everything for your good.
- You are quick to pray, since the almighty God is your Father who loves to listen to you and give you all you need.
- You regularly confess your sin to your Father, keeping your relationship close and enjoying his sure love and forgiveness.
- You are teachable and quick to submit to God, since you know his instruction and discipline are good.
- You love God.

In my life, the **child-of-God power** of the cross feels . . .

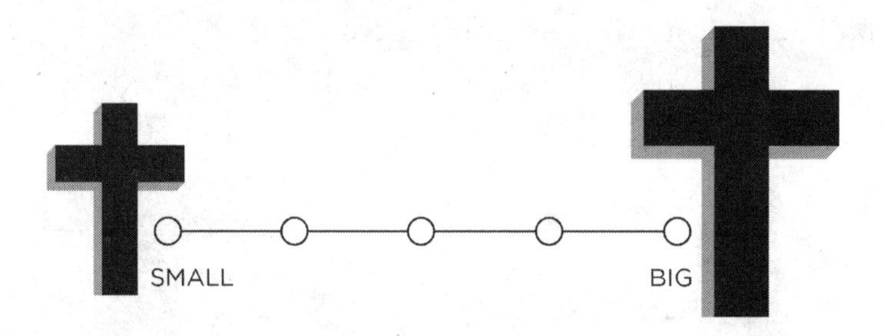

AREA 3: TRANSFORMING POWER

If you have faith in Jesus, his death is your death to sin and his life is your new holy life. By God's Spirit in you, you are freed from sin's control and are learning to be godly. You still have much growth ahead, but God is alive in you—and changing you. "Consider yourselves dead to sin and alive to God in Christ Jesus" (Romans 6:11).

A big appreciation for the transforming power of the cross in your life will mean:

- You have confidence that God is at work in you, so you fight sin even when it seems to have a firm grip on you. You don't just give in.
- You eagerly read and listen to God's Word because you figure it will pay off.
- You love hard-to-love people because you know the strength to do it comes from God.
- You know that *sinner* may describe you at times, but it is not your core identity. You are holy in Christ, and you want to live up to that.
- You stay close to God.

In my life, the **transforming power** of the cross feels . . .

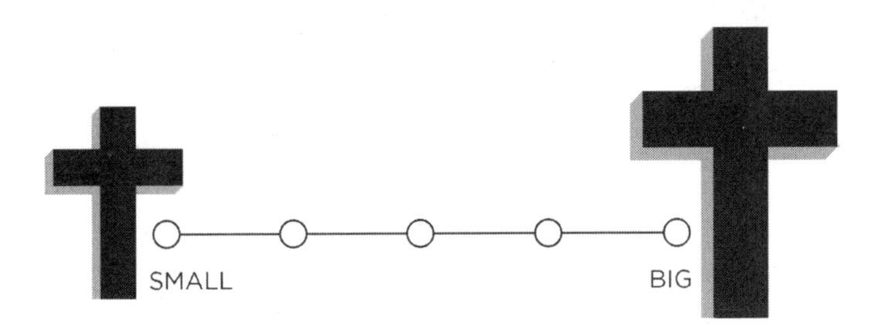

AREA 4: KINGDOM POWER

You now live for Jesus's kingdom, not for yourself. Jesus is calling people from all parts of the world. You join in that purpose. And you eagerly wait for his return, your own resurrection from the dead, a new heavens and new earth, and life forever with him. "By your blood you ransomed people for God from every tribe and language and people and nation" (Revelation 5:9).

A big appreciation for the **kingdom power** of the cross in your life will mean:

- You live for things that will last in the next world, not the things of this world.
- Your faith is about inviting others into God's kingdom, not just enjoying what he has done for you.
- You have a purpose: you love people who don't yet know Jesus, so that they too can experience his love and goodness.
- You do not fear death.
- All your hope is in God.

In my life, the **kingdom power** of the cross feels . . .

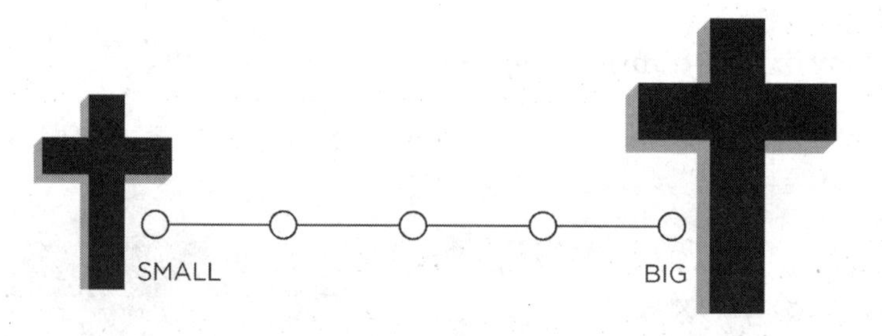

Share some of your ratings with the group, and explain what parts of the description caused you to give yourself that rating. Use an example from your life, if possible.

Where do you most want to grow, and how would this change your life with God?

What can you do to first grow in your appreciation for all Jesus has done, not just jump into trying to improve your behavior on your own?

WRAP-UP AND PRAYER *5 MINUTES*

As this study nears its end, pray that God would help you live a gospel-centered life. Pray that God would not just change your priorities in life, but that he would first deepen your love for Jesus.

Lesson

12

THE RISEN LORD

BIG IDEA

Jesus rose from the dead and ascended to heaven where he reigns today, having finished the task on earth his Father gave him.

BIBLE CONVERSATION *20 minutes*

With this lesson, we finish our study of Mark with an ending that shocked everyone who witnessed it, despite the fact that Jesus predicted it earlier in the book—three times! Have several people take turns reading Mark 15:40–16:20 aloud. Then discuss the questions.

You've probably heard about Jesus's resurrection before. But imagine you had just read about it for the first time and were surprised by it like the women were. What about the resurrection would seem most shocking to you, and why? What would be most thrilling?

What does Mark tell us to make sure we know that Jesus was really dead and really came alive again?

Why is it important that Mark makes sure we know Jesus died and really came alive?

One way to tell that a story sounds true is to look for details no one would make up or bother to include in a false story. What details in Mark's account of the resurrection give it a ring of truth?

****

Now read the article aloud, taking turns at the paragraph breaks.

PROP YOUR FEET UP

5 minutes

I once worked at a boys' summer camp. It was one of the greatest summers of my life. It was also one of the most challenging and hardest summers. Even knowing that, I would work there again in a heartbeat.

The days were long and busy. We would wake up early each morning and wouldn't stop until the evenings. We would lead activities like a ropes course, horseback riding, archery and marksmanship lessons, and much more. There was never a dull moment and most of the campers saw to that. They were loud and energetic, as boys tend to be, which made the days fun but exhausting.

Those in charge of the camp knew exhaustion and busyness were aspects of the camp, so they appropriately accommodated the camp counselors by giving them specific nights off. During one night off, several of these counselors had an idea. Keep in mind that these are twenty-year-old college guys. You might think they wanted to go out and party, but they went to a bookstore, found some comfortable chairs, and sat in silence. And according to them, it was beautiful.

You see, all the hard work done by these counselors rightly wore them out. They were doing good and important work—discipling young men. But that work also needed to be balanced with rest.

Along those lines, we read that "then the Lord Jesus, after he had spoken to them, was taken up into heaven and sat down at the right hand of God" (Mark 16:19). Jesus, in an infinitely more significant way, had been busy like we were at camp. He took on flesh and came to earth, he preached and taught constantly, he healed those afflicted with various illnesses, he cast out demons, he continuously resisted temptation, he perfectly obeyed his Father and loved his neighbor, he walked everywhere, he was beaten and crucified, he drank the cup of God's wrath, and then died. On earth, Jesus was . . . pretty busy.

But at the end of Mark, Jesus had finished his earthly ministry, having risen from the dead and is now seated at the right hand of God. Now he can prop his feet up because he accomplished the task his Father gave him. Scholars refer to this as Christ's "session." That word means he is seated and reigning.

We need to picture Jesus as a king, ruling on a throne. He did everything his Father desired of him—perfectly! He never sinned in thought, word, or deed. He perfectly loved his Father. He perfectly loved people, even his enemies. He did all of this and more. And now he has his feet propped up, so to speak, and is ruling the earth.

However, Jesus is not just out there in heaven somewhere far away. He also remains the Savior who draws near. This happened most clearly when he became a man and lived with us on earth. But even now that he is risen and ascended to heaven in his human body, he remains with us as God. Mark closes with that encouraging word: "And they went out and preached everywhere, while the Lord worked with them and confirmed the message by accompanying signs" (Mark 16:20).

The Word tells us that the Holy Spirit dwells in us and our body is his temple (1 Corinthians 6:19). It also tells us that our bodies are members of Christ; he is in us and we are united to him (1 Corinthians 6:15). The phrase *in Christ* is repeated throughout the New Testament. So as we end our study of Mark, we are reminded that although Christ is reigning and ruling in heaven, he is still with us in a very real sense.

Just as he appeared to Mary Magdalene to tell her he cares for her and remains faithful to watch over his children, we can be confident that we worship the same Savior. He is a loving and faithful Savior who remains steadfast and is with us today and tomorrow—to our last day or the day he returns.

DISCUSSION *10 minutes*

Do you tend to think of Jesus more as someone out there in heaven and far from you or as someone constantly near you? Why do you think about him the way you do?

How does it benefit you that the Savior who died for you now reigns over all things from heaven? How does believing this affect the way you live?

Lesson

BELIEVING THE RESURRECTION

15 minutes

When the Bible speaks of Jesus's resurrection, it often emphasizes how important it is to believe it truly happened. Even if you claim to believe it, you might struggle to live in a way that reflects your belief in something so remarkable. Consider some of what Jesus's resurrection means for you if your faith is in him:

- It means you too will rise from the dead someday. Your current life is not all you have to live for; it is barely the beginning. "We shall certainly be united with him in a resurrection like his" (Romans 6:5).
- It means you have victory over sin in your life. With God living and working in you, your destiny is to fight sin and one day be free of it completely. "Sin will have no dominion over you" (Romans 6:14).
- It means you have a real-time, personal relationship with a living Savior who loves you. "I am with you always, to the end of the age" (Matthew 28:20).
- It means any work you do to advance Jesus's kingdom or bring others to him has value that will last forever. "In the Lord your labor is not in vain" (1 Corinthians 15:58).

- It means all of God's promises to you are sure to come true. "All the promises of God find their Yes in him" (2 Corinthians 1:20).
- It means you have good reasons to be joyful and hopeful, no matter what happens in this life. "The sufferings of this present time are not worth comparing with the glory that is to be revealed to us" (Romans 8:18).

Keeping these truths in mind, dream about how believing the resurrection can impact your life. Take the time to think of some daily-life decisions that could fill in the blanks below.

For example, because Jesus rose from the dead, it makes sense for you to __**get to know him by studying the Bible**__ because __**you will meet him in person and be with him forever**__.

When you fill in the blanks, try to be specific and imaginative. Instead of saying it makes sense to *love others* because *it matters*, you might say it makes sense to *make friends with a lonely person in the lunch room* because *she might come to know Jesus and be your heavenly friend forever*. When you finish, discuss the questions at the end of the exercise.

How might the truth of the resurrection affect your PRIORITIES at school, at work, at church, at home, on teams, or when choosing activities, etc.? Be imaginative!

Jesus rose from the dead, so it makes sense for me to ______________________ ____ because ____.

How might the truth of the resurrection affect your RELATIONSHIPS with friends, family, strangers, etc.? Be imaginative!

Jesus rose from the dead, so it makes sense for me to ______________________ ____ because ____.

How might the truth of the resurrection affect your USE OF RESOURCES like your money, possessions, time, investment in others, etc.? Be imaginative!

Jesus rose from the dead, so it makes sense for me to ______________

____ because

____.

How might the truth of the resurrection affect your EMOTIONS when life is easy, when it's hard, when it's uncertain, etc.? Be imaginative!

Jesus rose from the dead, so it makes sense for me to ______________

____ because

____.

Share some of your thoughts with the group. Why do you think God gave you those specific thoughts? How might he be working in your life?

WRAP-UP AND PRAYER *5 minutes*

Our entire study in Mark should have helped you see how beautiful Jesus Christ is. If God has been working in you, you have been both convicted of sin and moved to hope. Pray now that you will see Jesus more and more. Pray that you would cling to the gospel daily, being reminded that Christ clings to you.

What are other ways we can pray? What are questions you have about the gospel? Please don't be afraid to voice concerns, doubts, or questions you have about Jesus.

Also, let's remember the last words of Christ recorded in Mark include "Go into all the world and proclaim the gospel to the whole creation" (Mark 16:15). Ask God to give you the strength, joy, and desire to tell others about Jesus.

LEADER'S NOTES

These notes provide some thoughts, mostly on the Bible conversation questions, from the author and editor who composed those questions. The discussion leader should read these notes before the study begins. Occasionally, the leader may want to refer the group to a point found here.

However, it is important that you NOT treat these notes as a way to look up the "right answer." In most cases, the best answers will be those the group discovers *on its own* through reading and thinking about the Bible passages and articles. You will lose the value of looking closely at what the Bible says and taking time to think about it, if you are too quick to turn to these notes.

LESSON 1: HERO OF HEROES

Jesus's authority is unlike any other human authority because he is the Son of God in person. On top of that, both of the other persons of the Godhead attested to Jesus's authority at his baptism. God the Father spoke from heaven, and God the Holy Spirit descended on Jesus. His authority to speak, heal, and conduct every other part of his saving work comes directly from God.

Jesus's authority showed up in all aspects of his ministry. He taught with authority, cast out demons with authority, healed the sick with great power, and called his disciples in such a way that they were eager to leave everything and follow him. His authority was accompanied by compassion and centered on helping others. Those who witnessed it firsthand found it astonishing. Jesus was not just a man of words; he had the actions and power to back up what he taught.

Early on, Jesus made it clear that he had an interest in calling sinners to himself and forgiving sins. This is his chief mission as the Savior. Predictably, those who did not see themselves as needy sinners resented this and opposed it. But those of us who know the depth of our sin can rejoice that, even today, Jesus uses his authority to call sinners.

Since Mark moves so fast, it's good to notice a few core truths about Jesus. He is God's Son (1:11). The gospel message he preached has two key points: repentance and belief/faith (1:15). And Jesus's fame is spreading both on earth and in the spiritual realm; the demons know who he is (1:24).

The exercise may get you to think about friends. Are they authorities over you? They may be. There could be certain friends who tell you to do certain things or who possess a certain level of power over you. Typically, every friend group has these dynamics. There are those in the group that are leaders and those that are followers. Without even realizing it, we often assume various roles with our friends and those roles are based on a certain understanding of authority.

Think about social media too. There are various rules and principles we abide by when we get on social media. Maybe there are certain pictures you won't post or other pictures you will post. Why do you post some pictures and not others? I would be willing to bet it is based on a certain authority. You realize that there are people out there who will approve or disapprove of those posts, so you are submitting to their authority without even realizing it.

LESSON 2: THE GREAT TEACHER

It's common for people to enjoy being part of the Jesus crowd but not really be very interested in Jesus himself or willing to let his teaching change how they live. Students, in particular, may join the Jesus crowd because their parents or friends are there, or because they like a youth leader. They may be there for the fun events or the feeling of belonging to a place. In these ways, they may be trying to use Jesus to get something else out of life.

Some of these reasons are not necessarily bad reasons to join the Jesus crowd. But with the parable of the sower, Jesus makes sure that those who are listening to his Word get challenged to take it into their hearts. He points us toward the best reason to hear his teaching: the fact that he is the best teacher ever, who loves us and gave himself for us as our Savior.

LESSON 3: THE COMPASSIONATE SAVIOR

Details in Mark 5 that show Jesus's compassion might include:

- He treated the demon-possessed man like a valued person by asking his name.
- He did not force himself on the people of the Gerasenes, but still sent them someone who would tell about him.
- He agreed to fight his way through a crowd in order to help the girl who was near death.
- He took time to stop for the woman who had the bleeding and to listen to her story, despite his busyness.
- He called the woman "daughter" and publicly announced that she was healed.
- The moment the father received bad news about his daughter, Jesus told him not to fear.
- Jesus kept his healing of the girl private and did not make a spectacle of her.
- He took her by the hand and called her by a tender name.
- He made sure she got something to eat.

For a man who can fix seemingly impossible problems, Jesus showed unusual humility. He did not get offended when the people of the Gerasenes asked him to leave. He also let the crowd outside Jairus's house laugh at him, and then brought the girl back to life quietly rather than making a show of it to prove himself right. Most powerful people don't have such an others-first attitude.

It is likely that both the demon-possessed man and the woman with the bleeding had been starved for human compassion until they met Jesus. Part of his kindness to them included not just healing them from their dishonorable conditions, but also giving them new assignments filled with honor: they were to tell others about Jesus. They had been spiritual and social outsiders, but they became insiders.

NOTE: You may wonder why Jesus insisted that both the demon-possessed man and the woman with the bleeding tell what he had done for them, but instructed those who saw him raise the girl to keep quiet about that miracle. Jesus probably was not yet ready to fully reveal the life-giving nature of his mission on earth and did not want the kind of attention that would have resulted. He also must have been thinking of the girl; he did not want her burdened with unwanted attention either. He gave each person he helped instructions that were most kind to them.

LESSON 4: THE ONE WAY TO OVERCOME SIN

The Pharisees saw themselves as people who were careful to be spiritually clean, but they failed to give enough consideration to the filth in their hearts. If they had, they would have rushed to Jesus to be made truly clean. We too might feel clean due to godly habits, like church attendance or Bible study. These are good things that are part of following Jesus, but a right assessment of the sinfulness inside us will lead us to Jesus himself as our only hope to be made clean.

Jesus's list of evils in the heart is humbling when we realize that, in some ways, it describes your heart and mine. When you see that list, do you want to push back and deny that some of these are present in your heart? Pride is in that list. Does your pride want to protest and say, "I know I'm sinful, but I'm not that bad." Jesus is teaching about the true nature of our hearts, not to beat us up but to point us to himself. Use the list not only to examine your heart but also to be grateful that, in Jesus, that list was nailed to the cross.

Peter may have been buying into the worldly idea that success means gaining power, receiving honor, and (certainly!) staying alive. But Jesus would later teach his disciples that greatness in God's kingdom comes by taking the role of a servant, and even by death (see Mark 10:43–45). Most believers are not called to give up their bodies to death for the sake of Jesus, but all of us are called to kill the sin inside of us and to put the needs of others ahead of ourselves. Forsaking lustful desires and selfishness really does feel like death—like you are giving up your source of life. But it brings deep joy and true life in the end.

LESSON 5: THE LOVER OF THE LEAST

Stories like that of the disciples' argument actually bring me great encouragement. When I see how childish and foolish they acted, I realize that God can use me too. The twelve disciples—whom Jesus chose—were arguing over who was the greatest. What a childish discussion that was! What Jesus did was brilliant. Not only did he confront their selfishness, he picked up a child as a visual aid to help them understand. Jesus was teaching that being great is not about being seen or worshiped by others; it happens by serving those who are weakest.

The disciples probably expected honor and recognition from others to come with greatness. In their culture, even everyday activities such as where one was seated at the dinner table or who walked first behind the teacher were determined by the order of greatness. This meant everyone could notice who was considered great and would treat those people with respect.

Children did not have a high status in that culture. No one would notice when a man welcomed or cared for a child, except maybe to wonder why he would stoop to a task so low. Jesus was teaching that being great is not about being noticed by others but about serving those who go unnoticed.

Self-sacrifice and suffering are part of Jesus's service to others, and so they show his true greatness. Jesus did not fight for the high place, but instead excelled at taking the low place. The Creator who is due all honor left his throne in heaven to live among his creation. He suffered the indignities of a sinful world. He spent his life caring for the needy and those no one noticed. He gave his life, on a despised cross, for sinners.

Our culture may not be as status-oriented as the one the disciples lived in, but we too tend to rate people by how important they are, how valuable they can be to us, and how it might look for us to be seen with them. For example, we might prefer friends who are funny—"I like them because they make me laugh." That can be a selfish thing, especially if we don't like other people because they aren't funny. We could be using our friends to feel good about ourselves or to look good to others. We must search our hearts on this.

The exercise calls for you to think about loving the least. Be sure to remember that Jesus Christ loves those who are considered least in his kingdom. He is the King who left his throne and came to serve those who were shunned by society. This is why, as his followers, we also reach out to the least in our community. We love and serve those who are often forgotten and unloved.

LESSON 6: THE KING BORN TO DIE

As he came into Jerusalem, Jesus embraced the role of a triumphant king who has saved his people. He rode into town, as a king might. He accepted the people's adoration and their shouts of "Hosanna," which are a reference to being saved. The people also spoke of King David, whose throne God had promised to establish forever (see 2 Samuel 7:16). Zechariah 9:9–17 is a prophecy about the King whom God had promised to send, and John 12:12–16 says Jesus's ride into Jerusalem was a fulfillment of that prophecy.

Jesus acted like a king too in the way he judged the fig tree and cleaned up his "castle" by driving out the people who were using it for business. He refused to be intimidated by others who thought they had more authority. Like a confident king, he didn't even feel a need to explain himself to them.

LESSON 7: OPPOSITION TO JESUS

It took courage for Jesus to tell a parable against the religious leaders while they were standing right there. Jesus was not afraid to point out the truth and to tell it forcefully, even when doing so was uncomfortable or would make people angry. Standing in front of the religious leaders, Jesus knew he was the Christ and the greatest of all prophets, and he acted like it. He is not one to back down in the face of evil, but rather fights evil.

It also took compassion for Jesus to do this. First, by confronting the religious leaders he was giving them one more chance to repent. He put their evil in stark terms so they might see what a horrible thing they were plotting and come to their senses. Second, by confronting the leaders in the hearing of the people, he was protecting the people from evil influences. Third, he was no longer sidestepping the leaders because he was ready to be put to death and to suffer for our sakes, which was the greatest compassion of all.

LESSON 8: THE COMING OF THE KINGDOM

The future Jesus spoke of in Mark 13 includes violence, political strife, and international crises. There will be extreme persecution of believers that involves heavy intimidation and pits family members against one another. False religion will seem to reign supreme, creating both physical and emotional suffering.

Jesus wants his people to be prepared to stand firm. Persevering through hard and dangerous times is a major theme of his talk, and this perseverance happens through trust in God. Believers must rely on the Holy Spirit who is in them, pray to the Father, remember Jesus for whose name they are being persecuted, and wait in hope for the return of the Son of Man. The evil forces will look strong for a time, but Christ is stronger and he will be back, in glory, to gather his people.

Although Jesus seems to have been thinking of particular events in history when he spoke of some of these trials, we can benefit from his teaching even if we do not figure out exactly what times and events he had in mind. His teaching is good instruction for any believer at any place and time until he returns.

There is an urgency in Jesus's closing parable about staying awake. We must be confident in God's grip on his children, that he holds us and keeps us and will take us home. And yet this gospel love and security should move us to have a certain alertness.

LESSON 9: LOVING THE UNLOVABLE

The woman who anointed Jesus understood his great purpose—that he had come to die—and was supporting him in it. In contrast, the others at the table were unaware, distracted, or unwilling to come alongside Jesus as he approached his time to die. She was supportive; they were unsupportive. She was aware; they were clueless or were trying to put it out of their minds. She was compassionate; they were uncaring. She was warm toward Jesus; they were coldly arguing about better things to do with the ointment. She was focused on *him*; they were focused on money.

Jesus did not have the full support of even his staunchest disciple during his trial. Leading up to Jesus's arrest, Peter was more interested in defending his devotion than he was in really listening to Jesus and taking his words to heart. At the most basic level, the dialogue between Peter and Jesus shows Peter correcting Jesus, the perfect Son of God who was predicting the future in this final week of his life. It's simply absurd. Mark tells us Peter was emphatic in his disagreement with Jesus, and even made sure he got the last word.

Yet Jesus didn't get angry and say, "Peter, I created the world, why don't you just shut your mouth, or I'll shut it for you." The Teacher was patient even with those who would deny him, and he continued to warn and correct Peter lovingly, right up to the moment he was taken away.

LESSON 10: THE SUFFERING SERVANT

Although Jesus did not sin in his fear and sorrow, already in Gethsemane he was dealing with a form of suffering that was deeply emotional, spiritual, and physical. Other accounts tell us Jesus was so distressed his sweat became like great drops of blood (Luke 22:44). He begged his Father to allow the suffering to be removed from him.

Yet his desire to avoid the suffering was not as great as his desire for his Father's will to be fulfilled through his suffering. Jesus went to the cross because he loved his Father and obeyed his God and because he loved us.

Before the cross, Jesus endured insults and physical beatings. Still, it may be that the greatest suffering during this time came from Peter. The leader of the apostles, the one who had been by Jesus's side from the beginning and claimed he would follow to the end, denied ever knowing him. That must have hurt. For our part, you and I should also realize our sin caused the cross. Jesus endured pain after pain after pain to pay for our sin too.

Although our own suffering might make us think we have an excuse not to obey God, Jesus's example shows us the opposite is true. Jesus's obedience was greater because he was willing to suffer in order to obey. Jesus embraced suffering because his obedience would not have been perfect obedience if it had been easy. A willingness to suffer for God shows we are truly obeying him rather than following selfish desires. Selfishness is not a reason to stop obeying, but a chance to prove we are obeying.

LESSON 11: THE FORSAKEN SON

Mark mentioned no evidence of Pilate finding any wrongdoing in Jesus. He reported that Pilate understood how Jesus's conviction before the chief priests was due to their envy, and that Pilate got no answer when he asked what evil Jesus had done. Mark also showed how mob justice made the entire proceedings unfair. Jesus was crucified because the chief priests stirred up the crowd, the crowd kept chanting, and Pilate wanted to quiet them. Perhaps the most extreme evidence of injustice is the fact that Barabbas, a known murderer, was released instead of the gracious life-giver, Jesus. This is the horror and also the beauty of the cross.

In addition to this unjust punishment, Jesus suffered a shameful death. The cross itself made dying in a dignified manner impossible, and Jesus suffered cruel mocking besides. The cross also represented a cursed death. Jesus's recitation of Psalm 22:1, "My God, my God, why have you forsaken me?" brings to mind the separation from God our sins deserve. And a death by hanging was a cursed death, according to Galatians 3:13. The tearing of the temple curtain, which was in place to keep God's presence separated from unholy people, shows that Jesus's death removed the curse and allows us to approach God.

Drinking the cup of God's wrath is beyond our hearts and minds. Yet Jesus became the forsaken one so we would be embraced. Now we may utter the word *Father* with confidence—because Jesus endured what he did. He obeyed his Father to the death so we can echo the words of the centurion: "Truly this man was the Son of God!" (Mark 15:39). Do not miss the picture of the centurion watching all this unfold before his eyes and drawing that conclusion. Let it add great strength to your faith; it is why Mark included it.

LESSON 12: THE RISEN LORD

NOTE: Bible scholars disagree over whether verses 9–20 of chapter 16 ought to be included as part of Mark's book. This study tells you to read that section, and the author's article refers to it. Whether or not the section is an original part of Mark, the ideas it expresses are repeated elsewhere in the Bible, so those truths have strong scriptural support.

Mark takes care to show that Jesus was really dead by mentioning Pilate's investigation and the centurion's testimony, plus the process of preparing Jesus's body for burial. The fact that Jesus really rose from the dead is also clear. Jesus's own words before he died attested to it, and the angel announced it after it happened. Then Jesus was repeatedly seen by person after person who had a hard time believing it at first, refused to accept it, but finally was forced to admit it was true—because it was undeniable.

The fact that the first witnesses to the resurrection were a group of women who had not even been mentioned earlier in Mark is the sort of element that suggests the story was not made up. Many scholars will say women's testimonies were not even valid in court in that society, making them a poor choice if one were making up a story and hoping it would be believed. If this were a lie, the liars would have lied better than this. But Mark carefully named the women—because they happened to be the actual people who really went to the tomb. He also included scattered details about their conversation, their reactions, the size of the stone, and the time of day.